Old School, New Clothes

Old School, New Clothes

The Cultural Blindness of Christian Education

RONALD E. HOCH
AND
DAVID P. SMITH

WIPF & STOCK · Eugene, Oregon

OLD SCHOOL, NEW CLOTHES
The Cultural Blindness of Christian Education

Wipf & Stock
An Imprint of Wipf and Stock Publishers
199 W. 8th Ave., Suite 3
Eugene, OR 97401

www.wipfandstock.com

ISBN 13: 978-1-4982-5939-2

Manufactured in the U.S.A.

Dedicated to Julianna, who is "far more precious than jewels." (Prov 31:10)

and

to the memory of David's mother—Barbara Jean Riggs Smith—the most courageous teacher he ever knew.

Contents

Preface

IN APRIL 1837, HANS Christian Andersen published "The Emperor's New Clothes," a tale in which two swindlers contrive a get-rich-quick scheme: they pass themselves off as weavers and convince the emperor to buy a glorious fabric made of a magical material that would be "invisible to anyone who was unfit for his job or hopelessly stupid." In actuality, no such material exists; the swindlers are simply selling the emperor a pretend fabric.[1] Once the emperor, who loves to follow the latest fashions, hears of this magical fabric, he orders the swindlers to make him a sample, and they pretend to weave the fabric on empty looms. The emperor, curious as to the progress of his fanciful new cloth, sends his trusted old minister to inspect the swindlers' work. When the minister arrives at the workshop, he is shocked, for he cannot see the fabric! This must mean that he is "unfit for his job or hopelessly stupid." Not wanting to lose his job or look foolish, he pretends to see the fabric: "'Well, what do you think of it?' asked the chap who was pretending to be weaving. 'Oh, it's enchanting! Quite exquisite!' said the old minister, peering over his spectacles. 'What a pattern and what coloring! I shall report to the emperor without delay how pleased I am with it.'"[2]

Eventually, the fabric is presented to the emperor himself. "'What's this?' thought the emperor. 'I can't see a thing! This is appalling! Am I stupid? Am I unfit to be emperor? This is the worst thing that could happen to me . . . "Oh, it's quite enchanting!" he said to them. "It has our most gracious approval." And he gave a satisfied nod, as he inspected the empty loom."[3]

The emperor then commands the swindlers to make a garment out of the pretend fabric, and a parade is organized with the express

1. Tatar, *The Annotated Classic Fairy Tales*, 270.
2. Ibid., 273.
3. Ibid., 274.

purpose of showing off the emperor in his new clothes. You can imagine the surprise of the townspeople when they see the emperor parading naked through the streets! Yet, not wanting to seem stupid or unfit for their jobs, the townspeople pretend to see the magical fabric, and give compliments to the king concerning his new clothes. Finally, a child in the crowd shouts, "But the emperor has nothing at all on!"[4] The townspeople, encouraged by the boldness of this child, throw off their folly and finally acknowledge that the emperor is parading around town stark naked. The emperor, feeling very bashful, does not want to admit his foolishness, and so he continues to parade around town naked while his chamberlains pretend to carry the train of his garment.[5]

The story, of course, highlights what can happen when people blindly maintain the status quo, or when the desire to follow the latest trend or fashion leads people to ignore the obvious. The title of this book—*Old School, New Clothes*—hints (not so subtly, perhaps) at our contention that most of what is considered Christian schooling today is suffering from a case of the emperor's new clothes. Many Christian schools purport to offer something new and exquisite but actually offer nothing more than the old, run-of-the-mill, non-Christian school; many Christian schools have adopted—indeed, are even founded upon—the same theological assumptions as non-Christian schools but do not realize or acknowledge it because it has become engrained in their culture, because it is status quo. Like the emperor, many Christian schools parade around claiming to have something innovative, new, or exquisite to offer, but in reality they are parading around in the buff—there is nothing innovative, new, or exquisite about them. The desire to follow the latest trends leads them to unquestioningly adopt certain philosophies and programs that contradict Scripture and undermine biblical discipleship.

Furthermore, just as the ignorance in the story extends from the emperor all the way down to the townspeople, the ignorance of prevailing theological assumptions reaches from the institutions training future Christian schoolteachers and administrators to the current leadership of Christian schools, as well as to teachers and parents. Many people are blindly maintaining the status quo, and with detrimental consequences. So, like the child who proclaims, "But the emperor has nothing at all

4. Ibid., 276.
5. For the full story, see ibid., 269–77.

on!" we hope to state what ought to be obvious, and perhaps help lead others out of blindness. Still, for the reasons that we will present in the following chapters, this blindness has not been obvious.

We will begin by defining the terms of the discussion and then trace the historical trends that brought us to where we are today (one of the "swindlers" in "The Emperor's New Clothes"?); that is, we will examine how and why Christian schooling has become so blind. We will then endeavor to expose the errors in the current theological assumptions that underlie much of Christian education today by showing the truth from Scripture (our version of exposing the emperor's nakedness). Finally, we will present an approach to Christian education that we believe is more faithful to the Scriptures than the current models—in other words, how right theological assumptions ought to flesh themselves out in practice and thereby shape both the teacher and the student.

At this point we must issue several important caveats. First, although we make certain judgments about Christian schooling, we are *not* making judgments about the intelligence or spiritual condition of those involved in Christian schooling. Christian school faculties are filled with brilliant, very committed, God-fearing individuals who are genuine believers in Christ. Second, the theological problems that underlie much of Christian schooling today, although widespread, are in no way all encompassing. There are some Christian schools that in important ways do not suffer from the problems that we outline here. Still, the presuppositions that control most Christian schools bear too close a resemblance to those that control their non-Christian counterparts. We are confident that what we present here will be beneficial for all Christian educators, so wherever you would classify yourself within this discussion—whether you are a teacher at a school that seemingly has it all together, an administrator who is struggling to discern what a Christian school ought to be and do, or a parent involved in homeschooling—we are certain that this book can (Lord willing) help you in your teaching ministry. At the very least, we hope that it generates a conversation that must take place so that God's people might be more faithful to their Lord. With that said, enjoy!

Ron Hoch and David Smith

1

Framing the Issue

*There are few phenomena in the theological world which are more
striking indeed than the impatience which is exhibited on every hand
with the effort to define truth and to state with precision the doctrinal
presuppositions and contents of Christianity.*[1]

—B. B. WARFIELD

DEFINING TERMS FOR A discussion or debate is not optional; it will
be done. The real question is whether the people involved in the
conversation will recognize the definitions they are using and have the
necessary abilities and patience to arrive at accurate definitions. People
may be unaware of the definitions with which they operate, but they
do not do without definitions. Unfortunately, the point that the great
Princeton theologian B. B. Warfield made over a century ago (see quote
above) has become the general fabric of much of American culture. It
has also found a welcome home within much of what identifies itself
with the Christian church in America, regardless of theological persuasion. In important ways it corresponds to Neil Postman's warning nearly
thirty years ago that Americans were amusing themselves to death.[2]
While Postman's thesis seems axiomatic to some communities, in others
it seems to have either fallen on deaf ears or not even been introduced.
None of this is surprising to those who know the central flow to Western
intellectual history. The basic route to how we arrived at this point will
be traversed in the next chapter, so we won't address it here. For now, we

1. Warfield, "The Right of Systematic Theology," 221.
2. Postman, *Amusing Ourselves to Death.*

begin with definitions of the most important terms and concepts in this discussion.

WHAT IS INTEGRATION?

In their "Series Preface: A Call to Integration and the Christian Worldview Integration Series," Francis Beckwith and J. P. Moreland established the parameters for the IVP series that seeks to help Christian college students "learn about and become good at integrating" their "Christian convictions with the issues and ideas in" their chosen majors and careers.[3] They rightly begin by defining the operative term *integration*. They identify two kinds of integration—conceptual and personal—that are seen from the following definition of the term *integrate*: "to form or blend into a whole," "to unite."[4] For Beckwith and Moreland, conceptual integration is when "*our theological beliefs, especially those derived from careful study of the bible, are blended and unified with important, reasonable ideas from our profession or college major into a coherent, intellectually satisfying Christian worldview.*"[5] They define personal integration as our seeking "to live a unified life, a life in which we are the same in public as we are in private, a life in which the various aspects of our personality are consistent with each other and conducive to a life of human flourishing as a disciple of Jesus."[6] Beckwith and Moreland affirm that these two kinds of integration are "deeply intertwined" and that "all things being equal, the more authentic we are, the more integrity we have, the more we shall be able to do conceptual integration with fidelity to Jesus and Scripture, and with intellectual honesty."[7]

What is conspicuous in their preface is that integration is defined and approached almost always as something humans *do*. We would argue that this reflects a fundamental error that both reflects and reinforces confusion on the matter. There may be some legitimacy to the idea that humans engage in some sort of integration. But as a human activity taking place in God's creation, it can be accurately understood only when viewed as subservient to and defined by the integration that

3. Beckwith and Moreland, "Series Preface," 9.
4. Ibid.
5. Ibid. Italics original.
6. Ibid., 10.
7. Ibid.

God created. Indeed, precisely because God created all things with an already existing integration, or harmony, it only confuses the matter when the term *integration* is used, first and foremost, as something humans *do*. Though we are not calling for the wholesale rejection of the use of the term to refer to something humans do, we would, at the very least, call for an approach that identifies integration in the intellectual realm as something humans, first and foremost, *discern*. Certainly we are to bring our thoughts into conformity with an already existing integration, so in that sense we can be said to integrate our thoughts with reality, or to *do* integration. However, getting the epistemological and historical order accurate here is no small thing precisely because the metaphysical belief that drives so much of the unbiblical thinking and living in the West reverses this order. It is in fact the relationship between what is going on internally with humans in their knowing and thinking and its relationship to what is external to us that is the fault line upon which one either embraces biblical thinking, or the Kantian (neo-Kantian) relativism controlling much of Western culture.

We concur with William D. Dennison:

> Christ's exhaustive and infinite wisdom creates, understands, interprets, and maintains the coherent wholeness of all things. This Biblical view of Christ's sovereign position as Creator underscores the comprehensive and coherent nature of his person and task as he brought all things into existence. . . . This integrative wholeness defines the context of the first male and female human beings (Gen 1:26–30). With integration as the *given*, the First Adam enters into differentiation (Gen 2:20). This constitutive relationship between integration and differentiation cannot be overstressed.[8]

Indeed, it cannot. It is also why it is right to say that theology is a constituent part of every branch of human knowledge. This is why years ago B. B. Warfield, while using the term *sciences* to refer to the various branches of human knowledge, stated the following regarding theology and its relationship to all branches of human learning:

> It [theology] is not so far above them, however, as not to be also a constituent member of the closely interrelated and mutually interacting organism of the sciences. There is no one of them all which is not, in some measure, included in it. As all nature,

8. Dennison, *A Christian Approach to Interdisciplinary*, 78–79.

whether mental or material, may be conceived of as only the mode in which God manifests Himself, every science which investigates nature and ascertains its laws is occupied with the discovery of the modes of the divine action, and as such might be considered a branch of theology. And, on the other hand, as all nature, whether mental or material, owes its existence to God, every science which investigates nature and ascertains its laws, depends for its foundation upon that science which would make known what God is and what the relations are in which He stands to the work of His hands and in which they stand to Him; and must borrow from it those conceptions through which alone the material with which it deals can find its explanation or receive its proper significance. Theology, thus, enters into the structure of every other science. [9]

This is where we can begin perhaps to see the basis of the problems regarding the whole project of integration, as that project is conceived and tackled by many within American Christian education. There is a failure to recognize the reality of the God-created, organic integration, and then think and act in accordance with that living organic integration. Notice that Warfield referred to the *organism of the sciences*.[10] Human knowledge and education are only rightly understood when we identify them as living organisms. We must therefore treat them and function within them in accordance with this living or organic character that has its existence, governance, and fulfillment in and through the Triune God. This has far reaching implications for how Christians ought to understand and function within educational endeavors.

METAPHYSICS, KANT, AND THE WORLDVIEW CONCEPT

Metaphysics is the study of reality. Along with the topics of theology, epistemology, anthropology, and ethics, it forms an important part of everyone's worldview. These five subjects are the way in which Ronald Nash categorized everyone's worldview. Nash defined *worldview* as "a conceptual scheme in which we consciously or unconsciously place or

---

9. Warfield, "The Idea of Systematic Theology," 68–69.

10. For more detailed understanding of Warfield's thought see Smith, *B. B. Warfield's Scientifically Constructive Theological Scholarship*; "B. B. Warfield, Systematic Theology and the Preacher's Task,"; Zaspel, *The Theology of B. B. Warfield*; Helseth, *"Right Reason" and the Princeton Mind.*

fit everything we believe and by which we interpret and judge reality."[11]
This is not the only way to define the term *worldview*, but it captures
all the essential features necessary for understanding the worldview
concept. The *term* worldview, or the German *weltanschauung*, as best as
can be discerned was first used by Immanuel Kant in his *The Critique of
Judgment* in 1790.[12] But as David Naugle rightly explains, the term was
soon used to "refer to an intellectual conception of the universe from the
perspective of a human knower."[13] Kant appeared to use the term only
once, but since it was joined to his view of knowledge that emphasized
"the knowing and willing self as the cognitive and moral center of the
universe" the worldview concept was used by his successors in European
intellectual life to advocate a view of knowledge that was not primarily
concerned to understand what the objects of knowledge are *in and of
themselves*, but *what they seem to be to us*. In other words, in this theory
of knowledge the individual's personal perceptions of reality came to be
the most important thing to consider when thinking about knowledge.[14]
One of the consequences of this was that it was not simply the differences in people's perceptions of reality that came to be important but
their willfully taking control of the object of knowledge so that their
conclusions about it corresponded to what they wanted.[15] Unfortunately

11. Nash, *Faith and Reason*, 24.

12. Naugle, *Worldviewt*, 58–59. Unfortunately and ironically, Naugle's emphasis
on the term *worldview* leads him to minimize the use of the *concept* in the work of
theologians leading up to and during the nineteenth century. While acknowledging
Calvin as the wellspring, Naugle praises James Orr and Abraham Kuyper as the source
of worldview thinking in the evangelical world. Perhaps Naugle's emphasis on the
term rather than the concept led him to miss the fact that the concept captured by
worldview was used among the Old Princeton theologians of the nineteenth century
long prior to James Orr and Abraham Kuyper. For the use of worldview as a concept
among the nineteenth-century Princetonians see Gundlach, "The Evolution Question
at Princeton, 1845–1929." This criticism should not deter one from reading Naugle's
overall helpful work.

13. Ibid., 59.

14. For summaries of the central features of Kant's philosophy see Frederick
Copleston, S. J., *A History of Philosophy* Volume 6 *Wolff to Kant*; Samuel Enoch
Stumpf, *Socrates to Sartre: A History of Philosophy*; Steve Wilkens and Alan G. Padgett,
Christianity and Western Thought: A History of Philosophers, Ideas and Movements
Volume 2 *Faith and Reason in the 19th Century*; W. Andrew Hoffecker, "Enlightenments
and Awakenings: The Beginning of Modern Culture Wars," 263–70.

15. As Kant stated, "'objects must be viewed as conforming to human thought,
not human thought to the independently real.'" Quoted in Robert W. Yarbrough, *The*

it is this Kantian, or its neo-Kantian modification, that controls not only the basic orientation to reality and knowledge in the West in general, but also much of the talk about integration among Christian educators.[16]

To approach the relationship between faith and learning, or theology and the knowledge of any subject discipline primarily from the perspective of needing to integrate them is to speak of these realities in a profoundly Kantian way. Faith and learning do not need to be integrated they *are* integrated.[17] We discern an already existing integration; we do not so much *do* integration as *discern* it. The terminological difference is very important. We need to learn how faith and learning *are* related. This is not simply a matter of semantics. Instead, it is a call for Christians in education to recognize: 1) some of the ways God-denying presuppositions have corrupted much of what passes for Christian education and schooling, 2) the centrality of theology for all human learning and living, and 3) the sanctification of the sinful educator for a truly Christian education.

ALL EDUCATION IS THEOLOGICAL

Since God is the creator of reality, all knowledge is theological. The subjects of epistemology (study of knowledge) and theology (study of God) are part of one another. In chapter three we scrutinize more closely their union by noting the central place of the doctrine of creation for a biblical view of God, humans and knowledge. For now we need to not only state that theology and epistemology are united but also that this union is clearly rejected by the prevailing neo-Kantian view of knowledge that controls Western academia. It can then be seen that it is an important

---

Salvation-Historical Fallacy? Reassessing the History of New Testament Theology, 75; See Dennison, *A Christian Approach to Interdisciplinary Studies*, 7-71 for a helpful analysis of how a Kantian and neo-Kantian theory of knowledge pulsates through the educational interdisciplinary project as that project has been conceived and pursued in the history of higher education in the West.

16. Douglas Sloan, *Faith and Knowledge: Mainline Protestantism and American Higher Education*.

17. One sees this same pattern of thought exhibited when Christians talk about *the need for the church to be unified* and are concerned to *work toward* unity. The biblical presentation is that the church *is* unified *in* Christ and *by* God. The individual Christian and the church corporately is to discern the nature of this unity and to be obedient to the imperatives placed upon us by it. Only in the latter sense can we legitimately speak of "working toward unity."

question to ask: To what degree can Christian educators and schools in forming their views of education and schooling take their lead, or seek to borrow, from non-Christian educators and institutions? The consequences of rejecting the union between theology and epistemology are, to say the least, numerous. Certainly one of them is the inability for even confessing Christian educators to present a coherent, dare we say it, *integrated* view of theology and knowledge. In other words, to the degree that confessing Christian educators follow the prevailing thought pattern of the West, to that same degree they fail to accurately discern and present the way theology and knowledge are already integrated. It is difficult to surmise how such putatively Christian education is going to impact the world with biblical thought and action.

THE SMELL OF KANT

When I (David) was in college, many of my classmates went to a small restaurant that served greasy and very tasty hamburgers. When you opened the door to the place its smell overwhelmed you and pulled you in. Who could resist the source of such an aroma? Not unlike thousands of other great eating establishments. Common to them all is the experience that the longer you stay in them the less you are able to detect their smell. It has become a part of you. Herbert Schlossberg expressed several years ago part of the problem that plagues many in the West, and we would add seems particularly acute among educators: "We do not see the environment, as Os Guiness says, because we see with it. That means we are influenced by ideas we do not notice and therefore are not aware of their effect on us. Or, if we see the effect, we find it difficult to discover the cause."[18] The problem that plagues many within Christian education and the American evangelical community in general is that the unbiblical ideas that govern academia and American culture as a whole have been largely accepted by them, and they are now significantly immune to detecting those unbiblical patterns of thought.

As they proceed in their preface to the Christian Worldview Integration Series, Beckwith and Moreland address the topic in a way that acquiesces to the prevailing unbiblical patterns of thought in the

---

18. Herbert Schlossberg, *Idols for Destruction: The Conflict of Christian Faith and American Culture*, 7. Could it be that this is a particular problem among those in allegedly Christian education because education as a distinct discipline in itself largely has its roots in an attempt to mediate an anti-Christian view of reality and human life?

West. They fail to condition their approach by God's sovereign Lordship over creation. As a result, and despite their genuine confession to the contrary, they regard that which is God's act and what already *is* as an activity humans must accomplish. When they do this they embrace the antithesis of what should be regarded as Christian. For example, the author's state, "*Christians hold that, when properly interpreted, the teachings of Holy Scripture are true.*"[19] One is left wondering: If not properly interpreted, are the teachings of Holy Scripture not true? In other words, the way they have worded the statement seems to suggest that *our* properly interpreting Scripture dictates whether the teachings of Scripture *are* true. They've worded it in such a way to reflect that humans create the truth validity of Scripture. But God and his word, the Scriptures, are true whether they are properly interpreted or not. Human comprehension and apprehension of the truth of Scripture does not determine whether Scripture is true. The statement is a clear confusion of categories that is done in a neo-Kantian pattern of thought.

At another place they state, "To live Christianly is to allow Jesus Christ to be Lord of every aspect of our life." Again, we have a confusion of what is and what humans do. Jesus is Lord. We do not give Jesus his Lordship. To be consistent with Christianity the statement would be better along the following lines: "To live Christianly is to willingly and self-consciously submit to Jesus and His Lordship." We readily admit and know all too well that this idea that Christians make Jesus the Lord of their lives is an extremely popular way of viewing the Christian faith. It is patently false. It reflects major confusion regarding the person and work of Christ and our place within the created order, and thus our relationship to Jesus. Jesus has all authority in heaven and on earth. He stated this very clearly to his disciples upon his ascension to heaven (Matt. 28:18-20). Jesus IS Lord. *We* do not *make* him Lord. Instead, we either submit to his Lordship resulting in salvation or we rebel against his Lordship, but in either case *we* are not *allowing* Jesus to *be* the Lord of any aspect of our lives. *He is Lord* of every aspect of our lives. We either discern his already existing Lordship or we don't. But either way we do not allow him to have that Lordship. Such confusion regarding the person and work of Jesus cannot help but touch upon their conception of the whole task of thinking about Christian education and this is revealed in further statements.

19. Beckwith and Moreland, "Series Preface," 10. Italics there's.

For Beckwith and Moreland, "[A]s Christians seek to discover and become excellent in their special vocation, they must ask: How would Jesus approach the task of being a history teacher, a chemist, an athletic director, a mathematician?"[20] In other words "What Would Jesus Do?" is presented as a helpful question in achieving the goal of the integration project and this in turn is seen as part of the attempt to "restore to our culture an image of Jesus Christ as an intelligent, competent person who spoke authoritatively on whatever subject he addressed."[21] How exactly confessing Christian educators are going to present Jesus Christ as intelligent and competent when they cannot rightly discern between the fundamental categories of being and doing and how this distinction relates to understanding the fundamental difference between us and God, we are not exactly sure.

It is the Protestant Liberal theology stemming from Friedrich Schleiermacher (1768-1834) and Immanuel Kant that summarized the Christian life in the question "What Would Jesus Do?"[22] This was the question the Social Gospel advocates of the late nineteenth-century saw as accurately expressing Christianity because they believed the latter was simply the product of what is in nature. They viewed the kingdom of God not as that which God brings to humans through his supernatural grace, but as what is simply brought by humans. According to this perspective, we bring God's kingdom simply by regarding Jesus as a wonderful teacher and supreme example to follow, and whose example can be followed simply because Christianity is nothing more than our expressing what is natural to us. This is what B. B. Warfield and J. Gresham Machen thoroughly exposed as unbiblical in the late nineteenth and early twentieth centuries.[23] Even confessing Liberal scholars such as Gary Dorrien readily admit that Protestant Liberalism and its Social Gospel is indebted to Kant and Schleiermacher, and is the attempt to conceive of Christianity as depending on only that which is internal to humans.[24] Beckwith and Moreland direct us down this same failed

20. Ibid., 12.

21. Ibid.

22. Some of what marks the historical development of this line of thought is surveyed in the next chapter so we will refrain from analyzing it further here.

23. B. B. Warfield, *The Collected Works of Benjamin B. Warfield* 10 vols.; *Selected Shorter Writings* 2 vols.; J. Gresham Machen, *Christianity and Liberalism*.

24. Gary Dorrien, *The Making of American Liberal Theology: Imagining Progressive*

path that embraces the metaphysical belief of Western culture and that proclaims there really is nothing to talk about but what we humans do, because we cannot get to what objectively *is*. It is not our conclusion that this is what Beckwith and Moreland truly believe or mean to advocate. Furthermore, we believe many other confessing Christian educators do not really believe these things either, yet it is what seems to be exerting significant control of the discourse on Christian education as seen from Beckwith's and Moreland's preface.

FOUNDATIONAL AND ORGANIC CONFUSION

To speak about *foundations* for human knowledge seems to bother a lot of seasoned scholars. They often associate it with a modernistic, rationalistic or Enlightenment approach to the topic. Some of these reservations are misplaced and due to the failure to distinguish between a basis for knowledge claims rooted in nothing more than human reason versus a basis that sees human reason as organically united to, and dependent upon God and everything in creation. Words mean what they mean based on how a speaker or writer uses them, and it is not automatically illegitimate to speak of *foundations* for human knowledge. Still, it would perhaps aid the discussion regarding knowledge if we shifted from speaking about it primarily from an inanimate metaphor, like the foundation of a building, to an animate or organic one, like the DNA of a living organism, as Warfield's treatment alluded to earlier suggests. While both are legitimate, the organic one we believe is more accurate to what Scripture teaches, and to what reality testifies. The central identifying feature of human knowledge forces one to see such knowledge as organically united to God as the creator Lord. From this perspective one can see that Beckwith and Moreland present a confusing picture of the organism that is human knowledge.

Beckwith's and Moreland's programmatic preface attempts to commandeer the early years of the church as presenting "Jesus to unbelievers precisely because he was wiser, more virtuous, more intelligent and more attractive in his character than Aristotle, Plato, Moses or anyone else."[25] To say the least, this is an interesting slant on and place to start when making one's first reference to the early church's proclamation of

---

Religion, xiii–xxiii.

    25. Beckwith and Moreland, "Series Preface," 12.

Jesus. While it is true that some in the early church affirmed that Jesus was more virtuous and wiser than Aristotle, Plato and Moses, this is only rightly understood as an aspect of the church's proclamation of Jesus as Lord. The Apostle Paul wrote in Romans 1:4 that Jesus was declared the Son of God by his resurrection from the dead. Jesus was proclaimed to be God himself and was presented as such by those theologians who were most influential in the development of church doctrine over the first several decades of her life, such as Irenaeus, Tertullian, Athanasius and Augustine. These men's primary concern was not to present Jesus as more virtuous, intelligent or more attractive (presumably intellectually and ethically) than Aristotle, Plato, or Moses. Instead, the biblical proclamation of Jesus that formed the center of the church's theology was that Jesus is the Second Person of the Trinity, the Lord of Glory, the creator of the cosmos, who has accomplished all that his people need for salvation and the redemption of the creation.[26] What is especially ironic regarding this point is that Beckwith and Moreland are attempting to communicate the need for Christians to have a "broader understanding of following Christ" and yet it is not until they arrive at their third reason for why integration matters that they make an attempt at speaking, at least conceptually, about creation and general revelation. It is the latter topic that is the central doctrine marking the DNA of a Christian view of human knowledge, and gives it its broadest conceptual category. Humans *are creatures* created in God's image and living in God's creation. While Beckwith and Moreland would doubtless agree with that statement their presentation fails to organize and express human knowledge as conditioned by that truth. What should permeate, direct, or condition the Christians thinking about all human knowledge is treated by them as a virtual afterthought.

If we are to proceed with a biblically faithful perspective on Christian education we should begin with the biblical doctrine of creation. Yet Beckwith and Moreland do not even mention this topic until the end of their third reason for why integration matters. The very topic with which God begins his written word, that frames the entire storyline of the Bible, and is thus, the doctrine that is the lodestar to guide

---

26. For some very good summary treatments of the earliest years of the development of doctrine in the church see J. N. D. Kelly, *Early Christian Doctrines*; Jaroslav Pelikan, *The Christian Tradition: A History of the Development of Doctrine, Vol. 1 The Emergence of the Catholic Tradition*; B. B. Warfield, *Studies in Tertullian and Augustine*.

our understanding of all other biblical doctrines, receives but a glancing swipe in their presentation. Virtually in passing the authors write, "[W]e must never forget that God is the God of creation and general revelation just as he is the God of Scripture and special revelation." They do not seem to recognize the intimate and organic relationship between general and special revelation, and that this relationship permeates all human knowledge.[27] Furthermore, they also fail to recognize that the terms special and general revelation are actually quite vague and are perhaps better understood to refer to natural and supernatural, or creational and soteriological (pertaining to salvation) revelation respectively.[28]

Their confusion is perhaps most acute when they attempt to establish that they are against a sacred/secular dichotomy, trying to fight against the bifurcation of faith and reason, and address the contemporary crisis in knowledge, all the while committing the aforementioned mistakes that are organically related to, and expression of, the dichotomy of faith and reason.[29] This can be seen in their decision to accomplish integration by using the term theology "to stand for any Christian idea that seems to be a part of a Christian worldview derived primarily from special revelation." This is so "there will emerge a number of different ways that theology can interact with an issue in a discipline outside theology."[30] Well that is just it. Strictly speaking, there are no disciplines "outside" theology, and theology cannot be considered at all apart from our place in the entire creation. Everything is theological. This is also why it is not just Christians who are engaging in theology. All humans, all the time, engage in theology, as long as one regards theology as referring to knowledge claims about God. By the very nature of the case, all human knowledge claims in any subject discipline are theological. It cannot be otherwise. This highlights that the relationship between the creation and human interpretation of the creation is one way of describing the organism that is human knowledge. When both the creature who is interpreting the creation and that creation are created and sustained

27. Warfield, "The Idea of Systematic Theology," 56; "The Biblical Idea of Revelation," 3-34.

28. For a treatment of the biblical doctrine of revelation from this perspective and that frames a Christian view of knowledge and redemption see B. B. Warfield, "The Biblical Idea of Revelation," 3-34; "The Idea of Revelation and Theories of Revelation," 37-48.

29. Beckwith and Moreland, "Series Preface," 15-19, 24.

30. Ibid., 24.

by God, then it will hardly do to construe the creature's interpretation of that creation as anything less than theological and moral. Our problem as sinners, and even redeemed ones, is that we always stand in need of discerning the theological character of: 1) all subjects, 2) the knowledge claims we make, and 3) ultimately everything we say and do. Beckwith's and Moreland's presentation in its most fundamental assertions acquiesces to the neo-Kantian pattern of thought that controls the vast majority of academic discourse not only in the non-Christian academy, but also, as their preface testifies to, even much of the putatively Christian academy.[31]

In *The One, The Three and The Many: God, Creation and the Culture of Modernity* Colin Gunton argued that the heartbeat of the *modern* perspective on reality and human knowledge is a disengagement of humans from nature. Humans treat the objects of knowledge as instruments, or "as the mere means to realize their will."[32] In other words, rather than thinking of and pursuing human knowledge in a way that sees humans as organically joined to nature, it thinks of and pursues knowledge in a way that fails to give full weight to our place within the natural or created realm. We detect this same modernistic smell not only in Beckwith's and Moreland's preface, but in much of what passes for Christian education. Our desire is to argue for a paradigm shift that forces anyone in education to own up to the theology that they are trying to perpetrate in the name of education, and to further recognize that the moral character of the knower governs all his or her knowledge claims. Thus, clarity or confusion regarding the biblical doctrines of creation and redemption will fully condition the knowledge claims and epistemological methods of humans.

Christians can only present a distinctly biblical view of education by thinking and acting in harmony with what God has already created and currently sustains. The work of Christian educators is not to try and do that which God has already done. The prevailing neo-Kantian perspective on knowledge that controls much of Western culture regards

31. George M. Marsden, *The Outrageous Idea of Christian Scholarship* endorsed this same approach by arguing that Christian scholars need to play by the rules set forth by the non-Christian academy. For how Marsden and several others have misunderstood and misrepresented Warfield's thought see David P. Smith, *B. B. Warfield's Scientifically Constructive Theological Scholarship*.

32. Colin E. Gunton, *The One, The Three and the Many: God, Creation and the Culture of Modernity*, 14.

humans as needing to do that which God has already done. This neo-Kantian view of knowledge gives controlling authority to the personally private perceptions of the individual and relegates religious and theological matters to a subjective realm disconnected from an objective realm of facts, reason and truth. Thus, the neo-Kantian view of knowledge presupposes a radical and fundamental disintegration between education and theology. Not only is this a theory that renders itself intellectually unsustainable by its own admission, but also is patently unbiblical. It has no place in a Christian view of reality and knowledge. Yet, it is this neo-Kantian view of knowledge that is entrenched in Western views of education. Because this neo-Kantian approach runs contrary to Scripture and creation, those who espouse it have a vested interest in ignoring and violating the latter two realities. Much of the dogma and methodology of Western forms of education express both this ignorance and violation of Scripture and creation. If Christians are to present a distinctly biblical way of thinking and living to non-Christians, then they must, among other things, articulate a distinctly biblical view of education and functionally adopt practices consistent with it. This has largely been neglected in much of what passes for Christian education in America. Instead, much of education by Christians in the West adopts the methodology and many of the mantras of those antagonistic to Jesus and his kingdom. We ought not to speak about needing to integrate faith and reason, or faith and learning, but rather needing to discern the integration that God created and illumines to us through his Word and Spirit. While many in the West may be confused about what marks the integration God created, including many confessing Christians, we believe that is, in important ways, the result of adopting beliefs and practices that, though widely popular, are nonetheless unbiblical. In what follows we seek to explain not only the fundamental roots of this unbiblical pattern of thought, but also to set forth a faithfully biblical view of and approach to education.

2

Surveying Historical and Theological Currents

[O]ur whole system of school and college education is so constituted as to keep religion and culture as far apart as possible and ignore the question of the relationship between the two.[1]

—J. GRESHAM MACHEN

IF WE ARE TO accurately understand the current discussion regarding the integration of faith and learning, we need some historical perspective on it and matters intimately related to it. Because God created humans in his image for the purpose of knowing him and in order to be fruitful, multiply, fill the earth and subdue it, learning is central to who we are and what we do. A Christian perspective on the integration of faith and learning affirms that its history spans all human history. Although it is beyond the scope of this work to trace that history in any detail, it is important to survey the primary shifts that have taken place in people's thinking in the West regarding the union of faith and learning. Since our concern as humans is to make knowledge, or truth claims, and put them into practice, the terms "knowledge," "truth," and "reasoning" are perhaps best understood when we recognize their organic union to what we learn and to all things we do. The subjects of metaphysics and epistemology are interrelated and part of everyone's worldview, and so the subjects of faith and learning and their history are intimately joined to people's thoughts about the nature of reality and how we think we know. The knowledge claims we make and our behavior are unavoidably related to who God created us to be. There is a union of being (metaphysics) and doing (ethics), but how the relationship between these realities

1. Machen, "Christianity and Culture," 2.

has been understood by various thinkers throughout the history of human thought in general and within the history of Christian theology in particular has differed.

General historical surveys, of course, are quite prone to oversimplification, and so they are always of limited value for a precise knowledge of the subject surveyed. Their necessity, however, reveals an important feature of human knowledge—that it is systematic and unitary. We are not content to simply gather a collection of data, and indeed we cannot, even if we wished. We simply cannot know by trying to consider the object of our knowledge in isolation from other realities. Anything we know, we know in relation to other realties that help form the basis of our interpretation of that object of knowledge. This dynamic is seen in every subject discipline. We are aided in our knowledge of the relationship between faith and learning when we understand the general historical flow of the conflict that has taken place in the West over the last millennium between faith and learning, or faith and knowledge.

While terminology, at times, can become a lightning rod, we will use the terms *premodern*, *modern*, and *postmodern* to identify the basic epistemological choices on faith and learning. In the end, we will argue that the terms *late-modern* or *hyper-modern* are better terms than *postmodern* for identifying the pattern of thought that controls much of Western culture today. The term *modern* does not refer to something that is current or up-to-date but rather to the philosophical beliefs regarding reality (metaphysics) and knowledge (epistemology) that were perhaps best, although not exclusively, expressed by Rene Descartes (1596–1650). The essential affirmation in those beliefs places the individual as the controlling authority in knowledge claims, and regards the personal perceptions of the individual as the ultimate determiner of knowledge. Premodern, modern, and postmodern also identify the epistemologies that have characterized to varying degrees people's beliefs and actions in the West for at least the last nine hundred years.[2] In order to benefit from this survey, keep in mind that these epistemological choices are not the product of natural forces working their inevitable consequences in human history. Instead, they result from several historical factors, not the least of which is the totality of willful choices made by humans

---

2. This is the basic template presented in Carson, "Dangers and Delights,"11–17, which is perhaps the best concise summary treatment of these epistemological matters.

responding to some of those factors. Thus, these matters integral to faith and learning run straight through the human soul and are unavoidably united to the empirical realities that mark people's lives. This affirms the union of theology, epistemology, history, and historiography (the writing of history), and affirms the union between the realities that are both external and internal to us.

ALL KNOWLEDGE IS THEOLOGICAL: THE BREAKUP

For centuries, it was generally accepted within the church that knowledge of any reality was united to knowledge of God. While this began to be questioned around the thirteenth century, challenge to it gained serious traction in Europe during the seventeenth and eighteenth centuries. By the beginning of the nineteenth century, an epistemology in the West had developed that in principle would fundamentally deny the objective reality of anything outside human perceptions, feelings, or intuitions. Although the implications of this philosophy, articulated most forcefully by Immanuel Kant, were not immediately experienced in the West, it resulted in the gradual decline and marginalization of a generally biblical worldview that controlled much of American public life throughout the nineteenth century and in the early twentieth century. This decline and marginalization has accelerated perhaps most significantly because of developments in industrialization, technology, and transportation. It is often identified as leaving the West a "post-Christian" culture.[3] Among the many results of this epistemic revolution has been the acceptance of the idea that humans must determine reality, not discern it. In other words, humans are thought of as needing to do what God has already done. Thus, one of the ways in which one can see how many Christian educators and theologians are under the sway of a fundamentally unbiblical and God-denying worldview is that they approach the integration of faith and reason, or faith and knowledge, from the presupposition

---

3. Although there is some legitimacy to this name, it seems to suggest that there was a time when one could identify the West as "Christian." That is questionable, to say the least. We believe that the most accurate way of thinking of the West since the Protestant Reformation is that it has been marked to varying degrees and ways by both Christian and non-Christian principles. Thus, we consider it a serious historical, theological, and philosophical mistake to think of any time period in the West as "Christian." Still, we recognize that not all uses of the term *post-Christian* necessarily imply that there was a time in the West when it was fully Christian.

that these realities *need to be integrated*. This chapter is meant to help the reader see the general historical currents in this epistemic revolution.

"PREMODERN" EPISTEMOLOGICAL EMPHASES

A premodern epistemology primarily marked Europe from 1200 to 1600 AD. A premodern epistemology affirmed that the God of Scripture has all knowledge and reveals himself by his Word, both written and made flesh. Creation, as a product of God's Word and Spirit, was regarded as revelation from God, but one needing to be interpreted by God's written word. The primary vehicle through which God dispenses this knowledge to humans is his church, or his redeemed people. Human knowledge from a premodern perspective is a subset of God's knowledge. By this affirmation, one endorses the belief that human reason is an inherently "faith-based" operation, that human reason is inherently religious. Central to recognizing that human knowledge is a subset of God's knowledge was acknowledging that the Bible taught that God created humans in his image with knowledge and the capacity for more. While church authorities throughout history have differed over how much humans can know truly from each means of revelation—creation and the written word—and how these means of revelation related to the church, they nonetheless agreed that God knows everything. Again, from this perspective, human knowledge is a subset of God's knowledge, and humans can know truly because of who God is and what he does. [4] Still, during this premodern era some regarded human reasoning as divorced from faith commitments. Such thinking was not the product of historical events peculiar to the late medieval era, or of any particular era of history, but rather of the affirmations of the human soul in rebellion against God. Thus, the disintegration or disconnect between faith and reason that exists in people's thinking is fundamentally a manifestation of sin. Although it is perhaps helpful to some degree to identify historical circumstances that may have fostered the popularity of thinking that human faith commitments are, or can be, disconnected from human reason, no historical circumstances *by themselves* caused this separation, or can cause it. [5]

---

4. Carson, "Dangers and Delights," 12.

5. One of the significant problems that plagues allegedly Christian historiography is the acceptance by many Christian historians of historicist presuppositions. As a result, many Christian historians analyze and draw conclusions about historical events,

"MODERN" EPISTEMOLOGICAL EMPHASES DEVELOPING
IN THE "PREMODERN" ERA

During the medieval era (approximately 400–100 AD) and moving into the Middle Ages (approximately 1000–1300 AD), the primary concern of pastors and theologians "was the justification of faith to reason," or the attempt "to harmonize reason and faith."[6] In other words, many considered human reason, and by implication human knowledge, as not pervasively conditioned by faith commitments.[7] It seemed that some were considering faith as something added to reason, not as integral to it. It was becoming more acceptable for theologians and other scholars to think that there were truths accessible to us simply through reason and apart from any faith commitments. Whereas the great theologians Augustine and Anselm had believed that the Christian has "faith seeking understanding," some in the medieval era began to operate according to the inverse of this dictum.[8] Such intellectual developments were in organic union with developments in the relationship between the church and state.

---

people, and ideas according to the belief that only naturalistic explanations are worthy of the academy. See "The Link: Christian History Today," 51–54; Seeman, "Evangelical Historiography Beyond the 'Outward Clash'" 95–124. Unfortunately, prominent historians George Marsden and Mark Noll have largely acquiesced to the dogma of the non-Christian academy in the way that they write history. Even some non-Christians recognize that the historical record, and not scholarly communities, imposes itself on human interpretations of that record. See Evans, *In Defense of History*, 89–110. Evans, 99, rightly criticizes Appleby, Hunt, and Jacobs, *Telling the Truth about History*, for failing to recognize that "the past does impose its reality through the sources in a basic way," and asserting that the authority for interpreting the past is grounded in a community of scholars. As Evans writes, "Good rules transcend scholarly communities and do not therefore depend on their acceptance by them." This latter statement directly contradicts Marsden's idea that Christians ought to play by the same set of rules as non-Christians in academic work. See Marsden, *The Outrageous Idea of Christian Scholarship.*

6. The first quote is from Warfield, "Apologetics," 18. The second quote is from Leff, *Medieval Thought*, 19.

7. Ibid; Leithart, "Medieval Theology and the Roots of Modernity"; Pelikan, *The Growth of Medieval Theology (600–1300).*

8. Leithart, "Medieval Theology and the Roots of Modernity," 153.

CHURCH AND STATE: PICTURING
THE FAITH/REASON UNION

The emperor Constantine had wedded church and state in 313 AD, and this union led to various degrees of corruption both in the church and state. This corruption induced many to question the validity of that union. The union of church and state had an analogous relationship to the union of faith and reason in the intellectual sphere. This is not to say that people were consciously aware of this analogous relationship. As the corruption that took place between the union of church and state became more pronounced, people began to question not only the validity of their union but also the corresponding union of faith and reason. In other words, people began to ask: If the church and state ought not to be united, might it be that there is a sphere in which faith is disconnected from reason, or in which reason can operate outside of faith? Increasingly, throughout the medieval era, human reason and the civil authorities began to be viewed as having their own sphere of authority independent of religious faith and the church.

The work of Thomas Aquinas (c. 1225–1274) was central to the medieval era. The controversy surrounding Aquinas swirls around the question of whether his writings affirm either explicitly or implicitly a separation of or a synthesis of faith and reason. That is, did Aquinas, through his adoption (seemingly from Aristotle) of various ideas and methods, advocate that non-Christian reasoning can operate within its own legitimate domain and produce a system of knowing independent of faith commitments? Did Aquinas reject the idea that human reasoning is by its very nature a faith-based or faith-conditioned enterprise? As it is with most theologians who wrote extensively, there are passages within Aquinas that seemed to lead to contradictory answers. Regardless of how these things were precisely understood by Aquinas, his writings have been used to endorse the assertion that humans can acquire true knowledge apart from faith commitments. Thus, the way he was interpreted, at least by some, reinforced the idea that the domain of physical and intellectual activity of the church should be thought of as disconnected in meaningful ways from the physical and intellectual activity of those outside the church. It just so happened that the great majority of people wanted to be included in the church in the thirteenth century, so this disconnect or dualism between church and state, faith and reason, grace and nature, did not reveal itself in a prominent way during the thirteenth century. Still, like a seed germinating under the earth, this dualism would only need more time and the right conditions in order to grow and produce fruit.

Considering human reason as separated from religious faith of any kind would eventually be used by both church and state authorities to argue for each having a sphere of authority untouched by the other. Of course, it became painfully obvious in Europe during the fourteenth through sixteenth centuries that neither the church nor the state was satisfied with the other operating solely within its own sphere, disconnected from the other. The church resided in particular geographic territories that had to be governed by civil rulers in accordance with a particular law. Although some civil rulers certainly were concerned, for personal and/or religious reasons, to maintain good standing in the church, even those who were not so concerned understood the strategic political benefit of at least having the public appearance of good standing in the church. Significant numbers of rulers in each realm wanted to use the other realm to their advantage. In other words, the reality of their interconnectedness was viewed by some civil and ecclesiastical authorities as something to exploit for their benefit. Throughout the Middle Ages, a person's standing in the church had enormous influence upon his or her economic, political, and social relations. So, while some theologians and philosophers could speculate about the distinct relationship between faith and reason, the social, political and church scene embodied a relationship between religious faith and human reason that saw the two as intricately enmeshed in each other. But this enmeshment in people's thinking would begin to disappear as the Reformation took root and religious wars ensued.

Church Reformation, Religious Wars, and the Elevation of Reason

The stakes during the Reformation period were life and death. Too much power hung in the balance for church and civil rulers to sit idle and listen to Martin Luther and others undermine centuries of established order. Although it is virtually impossible to trace all the relationships of cause and effect between people's beliefs and actions, one thing is certain—people on both sides of these issues were willing to die and kill for their beliefs. In fact, by the time the Thirty Years' War concluded in 1648, Europe had to face the fact that it was literally killing itself over matters regarding faith and reason. Whose faith? Whose reason? It was during the midst of this frighteningly intense conflict that the French Catholic scholar Rene Descartes promulgated his now famous statement, "I think, therefore I am."

Most scholars recognize the modern era in epistemology as beginning with Descartes, even though his express concern was to bolster Christian belief, not to undermine it. Yet, what Descartes affirmed, or how others used what they thought he affirmed, was not substantively different from what had been embraced by men and women since the earliest days of Greek philosophy. It was aptly expressed by Protagoras (c. 485 – c. 410 BC) in the fifth century BC: "Man is the measure of all things."[9] In turn, the Bible warrants us to recognize that this is the essence of sin—the exaltation of humans that amounts to our adopting the arrogant notion that we can rightly interpret reality based solely on the use of our senses and reasoning. For this reason, it is not biblical to try to identify the source and nature of modernism as a philosophy in simply the circumstances of a particular historical era, or the activities or ideas of a particular person or group of people in history. Though one can find some who blame Luther for this exaltation of human reason and the individualism that now marks Western culture as a whole (and that came to be identified as *modernism*), one cannot find in Luther's thought the justification for such rationalism and individualism. Luther and Calvin in particular insisted that human reason was the creation of God, and must be brought into submission by and to God's Word and Spirit in order for humans to rightly know.

Long before Descartes, epistemological modernism had been percolating in Europe. So, though it is useful to recognize that beginning around the mid-seventeenth century an increased emphasis upon an epistemological modernism marked particular academic sectors of European life, we go fatally astray if we think that this modern epistemology, with its emphasis on the individual, was new to human history during the Reformation or post-Reformation periods, or simply the result of things going on during those times. What was new regarding it during seventeenth-century Europe was the degree to which it undermined the epistemic authority of God's Word for knowledge claims. When the presuppositions of a modern way of knowing were used to

9. Stumpf, *Socrates to Sartre*, 32.

alter biblical scholarship, the primary revolutionary means to alter the worldview of people in the West was born.[10]

MODERN BIBLICAL CRITICISM
AND THE "FACT/VALUE" DIVIDE

While the premodern epistemology regarded human knowledge as a subset of both God's knowledge and his activity, the modern way of knowing reversed, in important ways, this premodern order. In concert with Descartes' work came developments in the study of Scripture that produced what is called Modern Biblical Criticism. Such criticism is rightly called *modern* because in significant ways it relies upon and is the application of a modern epistemology. Such epistemology is based on the belief that the only reality to which humans have access is measurable by our five senses. In this we see that a modern view of knowledge is organically related to philosophical naturalism, or the belief that nature is all that exists. Such naturalism is perhaps best expressed in Carl Sagan's famous aphorism, "The cosmos is all that is, ever was or ever will be." When viewing the Bible from the perspective of a modern way of knowing, one must regard it as simply the product of natural forces or circumstances. Thus, the study of history through this naturalistic lens controls the view one has of the Bible. Also, one can see that this simply begs the question regarding a view of God as the creator who is both the source and sustainer of all aspects of creation, and thereby providentially in control of human knowledge and living.

The first two seminal practitioners of the historical-critical method were Baruch Spinoza (1632–1677) and Richard Simon (1638–1712). Rather than thinking of the Bible as God's supernatural work in which he governed human events and its human authors in order to produce the text, the Bible was regarded as merely the product of humans.[11] The

10. Kuklick, "On Critical History," 57. Kuklick argues that the historical-critical method has been more influential in shaping the worldview of people in Western culture than any other development in the past several centuries, including Darwinism.

11. A biblical view of the production of the Bible affirms the union of God and humans, the supernatural and the natural. For perhaps the clearest and most concise explanation of these points, see Warfield, "God's Providence Over All," 110–15; Warfield, "The Divine and Human in the Bible," 542–48. For the history and character of modern biblical criticism, see Brown, *The Rise of Biblical Criticism in America, 1800–1870*; Harrisville and Sundberg, *The Bible in Modern Culture*; Frei, *The Eclipse of the Biblical Narrative*; Linnemann, *Historical-Criticism; Is There A Synoptic Problem?*;

biblical writers were seen as interpreting their historical circumstances through a religious mindset that was simply a product of natural circumstances. The historical-critical method reveals its modernist bent in its presumption that humans can attain to an absolute certainty by simply relying upon their five senses and their ability to reason. Thus, this epistemic certainty is tied to the employment of a particular method. So, if humans will just exercise sufficient "rigor and control" in their method, they can attain an absolute certainty in knowing.[12] The historical-critical scholar is certain that his or her method will deliver true knowledge of the Bible.

Throughout the eighteenth and nineteenth centuries, biblical scholars, pastors, philosophers, and literary figures built upon Spinoza's and Simon's groundbreaking work. They used modernist beliefs to revolutionize the understanding of the Bible. Central to understanding the character of a modernist epistemology is to recognize that it is wedded to a metaphysic, or view of reality, that divides reality into two fundamental categories. This is called the "Fact/Value" Split or Divide. Perhaps the table below will help in understanding it.

"The Fact/Value Divide": Terminology and Concepts

Facts	Values
Empirical Data	Personal Experience
Object and Objectivity	Subject and Subjectivity
Reason and Rational Discourse	Faith and Feelings
Science, Knowledge, and the Intellect	Spirituality
Education and Scholarship	Religion and Theology
Politics	Worship
Public Policy	Ethics
Government and Laws	Interpretation
Public	Private

What became increasingly clearer throughout the eighteenth century regarding these matters united to modern biblical criticism and epistemology was that the only way to speak meaningfully about reli-

---

Biblical Criticism on Trial; Maier, *Biblical Hermeneutics*; Scholder *The Birth of Modern Critical Theology*.

12. Carson, "Dangers and Delights," 14.

gion, theology, and/or spirituality was to place them in the subjective or values domain. Throughout the history of human thought it has been recognized that in order to understand and explain human knowledge one must do justice to the relationship of the object known to the subject who knows that object. Every educator, regardless of the subject he or she teaches, ought to have clear competence in explaining the fundamental issues on the relationship between the objective and subjective elements in epistemology. As explained in chapter 1, since God is the creator of both the knowing subject—humans—and all the objects we could know, all human knowledge is pervasively theological. Thus, a biblical view of knowledge affirms that there is an organic relationship between the objective and subjective elements in epistemology, because God who created all things is truly revealed in the objects he created or has providentially allowed to exist.[13] It is precisely this belief in the union between the object known and the subject who knows that is fundamentally denied by a modern view of knowledge. This can be seen, among other places, in Spinoza's affirmations on the relation of theology to philosophy and reason.

In what is likely his most significant work, Spinoza wrote that "theology is not bound to serve reason, nor reason theology, but that each has her own domain. The sphere of reason is, as we have said, truth and wisdom; the sphere of theology is piety and obedience."[14] Moreover, he asserted that theology "defines the dogmas of faith . . . only in so far as they may be necessary for obedience, and leaves reason to determine their precise truth."[15] In addition, "philosophy should be separated from theology, and wherein each consists; that neither should be subservi-

---

13. Contrary to much of the prevailing story line, the Old Princeton theologians were not the ones who facilitated the acceptance of a modern view of knowledge. B. B. Warfield in particular was the one who articulated how the objective and subjective elements in knowledge are united. He resoundingly rejected the "Fact/Value Split." Unfortunately, this faulty view of the Princetonians, which is organically united to a faulty analysis of several intellectual currents, has been popularized by numerous scholars and repeated by Pearcey, *Total Truth*. For an accurate assessment of Warfield's beliefs and those of the Old Princetonians, see Helseth, *"Right Reason" and The Princeton Mind*; Smith, *B. B. Warfield's Scientifically Constructive Theological Scholarship*; Smith, "B. B. Warfield, Systematic Theology and the Preacher's Task"; Zaspel, *The Theology of B. B. Warfield*.

14. Spinoza, *Theologico-Political Treatise and A Political Treatise*, 194.

15. Ibid.

ent to the other, but that each should keep her unopposed dominion."[16] It was this endorsement of a "fact/value" split in the modernist way of knowing that became entrenched not only within certain forms of biblical scholarship throughout the eighteenth and nineteenth century but also within Western culture as a whole. The philosopher Immanuel Kant and the theologian Friedrich Schleiermacher helped solidify its entrenchment.

PROTESTANT LIBERALISM AND THE FLIGHT FROM EXTERNAL REALITY AND AUTHORITY

Immanuel Kant was a Prussian-born philosopher whose writings came at the end of the Enlightenment, a period that stressed the modernist epistemology. In summary, Kant was concerned to emphasize human limitations in knowing. He especially expressed what could and could not be considered legitimate objects and methods of knowledge. Fundamental to Kant's theory of knowledge was his distinguishing between what he called the "phenomenal" and "noumenal" realms, as well as "practical" and "pure" reasoning. Kant's theory denied that humans could have knowledge of reality, or the truly real. In principle, Kant denied that we could have knowledge of the essential nature of things. The result was a shift from speaking in terms of what things *are*, to speaking in terms of what things *appear to be to us*. In philosophical language this meant an undermining of the topic of metaphysics. As John Frame, systematic theology professor at Reformed Theological Seminary, has stated, "In the history of thought, we live in a distinctly anti-metaphysical age. The philosopher Immanuel Kant (1724–1804) provided a powerful impetus toward metaphysical skepticism, as he tried to show that traditional metaphysics, whether philosophical or theological, was all speculation that went beyond the proper limits of human thought."[17]

According to Kant, all human knowledge is limited to "the world of experience," and so what we call knowledge is also limited by the way in which our minds interact, perceive, and organize the data of our experience.[18] Necessary to Kant's theory was his belief that the data of our sensory experience, what he called the phenomenal realm, was to

16. Ibid., 198.

17. Frame, *The Doctrine of God*, 214.

18. Stumpf, *Socrates to Sartre*, 309.

be distinguished from and considered as separated from the noumenal realm. The latter would allow us to know what a thing is in itself, or its essential nature. Integral to this distinction was his belief that God, the cosmos, and the self were not true objects of human knowledge, but were realities that we had to have a conception of in order to reason. Of course, how precisely Kant could know that humans could not truly have access to what things are in themselves—or could not know God, the cosmos, or the self—is a serious problem with his theory. In order to rightly identify a reality so that you might say you do not know it is to contradict yourself. One obviously knows something about it—you can at least name it, and that name corresponds meaningfully to what you know it to be. The problem lies in Kant failing to distinguish between a belief or faith commitment versus uttering a truth claim that he claims is true for everyone, for all times and places. Furthermore, there were theologians and philosophers in the nineteenth century who argued this same point against Kant.[19] These arguments that questioned Kant's most basic presuppositions were not so much refuted as *willfully ignored*. The result was that many theologians, philosophers, and scholars in every subject discipline throughout the nineteenth-century adopted Kant's humanistic and relativistic philosophy that allowed the individual to be the controlling authority in knowledge claims, as knowledge came to be thought of as the private perceptions of each person.

Though Kant might not have endorsed some of the radical skepticism that has become associated with his philosophy, he nevertheless embraced it in principle. Kant's theory taken to its logical conclusion means knowledge is not the discovery or discernment of realities that had their own distinct metaphysical status. Instead, human knowledge was considered to be the interpretation that we have of our experience, as we bring our categories of thought to organize and make sense of our experience. Rather than thinking that the objects that we know have a status or quality to them that obligates us to think about and respond to them in a particular manner, a Kantian way—or what some call a neo-Kantian way—of knowing virtually removed all objectivity of any kind from knowledge claims. What Kant affirmed in epistemology, Friedrich Schleiermacher applied in theology, thereby helping reconceptualize Christianity. His reconceptualization relegated religious claims to a

19. McCosh, "Recent Works on Kant," 425–440.

private, subjective sphere so that they were considered outside the influence and evaluation of a public and objective sphere.

According to Colin Brown, Schleiermacher is to liberal theology what Darwin is to modern biology; they are "founding fathers."[20] Gary Dorrien, who praises modern Protestant Liberal theology, identifies Kant and Schleiermacher as its source, and regards it as "the idea of a genuine Christianity not based on external authority."[21] The view of the Christian faith represented by Schleiermacher and Protestant Liberal theology sees Christianity as fully explained by natural factors only, and relegates it to a private and subjective realm of feelings.[22] He considered that the "religious consciousness" of the believer was the "the proper subject of theology."[23] Schleiermacher went so far as to affirm, in direct contradiction of the Apostle Paul in 1 Corinthians 15, that it did not matter for Christian faith whether Jesus rose bodily from the grave. For Schleiermacher and Protestant liberal theologians, Christianity was viewed as the product of purely material or natural forces.[24] Thus, the principle regarding history and the explanations of Christianity by Protestant Liberalism are the same as those controlling the mainstream academy, as well as some of the academic work of confessing Christians. The beliefs that Kant and Schleiermacher endorsed led to a view of religion in general and Christianity in particular that saw these as not about

20. Brown, *Jesus in European Protestant Thought*, 110.

21. Dorrien, *The Making of American Liberal Theology*, xxi–xxiii. The quote is found on p. xxiii.

22. Contrary to Tillich, *A History of Christian Thought*, 388–400, one can hardly root this conclusion simply in Hegel. See Gerrish, "Natural and Revealed Religion," 662, who writes that for Schleiermacher, "religion is not correct belief, nor correct behaviour [sic] either, but the poetic expression of lively feeling." Further, "The essence of religion is an elemental 'feeling' or 'intuition,' and our access to it is by observing the structure of consciousness—in the final analysis, our own consciousness," 663.

23. Quote is from Dorrien, *The Making of American Liberal Theology*, xvi; cf. Brown, *Jesus in European Protestant Thought*, 131–32; Wilkens and Padgett, *Christianity and Western Thought*, 13–21.

24. Warfield, "The Idea of Revelation and Theories of Revelation," 38; Brown, *Jesus in European Protestant Thought*, 130, quotes Schleiermacher regarding the importance of the bodily resurrection of Jesus for the Christian faith: "[O]nce the act of dying had taken place in its spiritual significance, whether the physical part of death had been completed or not seems to me to be of no importance whatever." On that basis, what relevance does Jesus have for the material world?

believing a set body of doctrinal beliefs, but about feeling and actions.[25] Of course, once one assumes that there is no reality accessible to us that we can say corresponds to what objectively *is* for everyone—no reality that we can set our mind upon and to which we can and should conform our thinking—one has introduced a virus that has the potential to cause people to be obsessed with feelings and actions, and simultaneously to have little or no ability to intellectually critique those feelings and actions. This confuses the relationship between *being* and *doing* and has greatly influenced an overemphasis on *doing* to the detriment of *being*.

The beliefs that controlled Schleiermacher's perspective on the Christian faith and that governed the development of modern Protestant Liberal theology have been alive and influencing the development of certain sectors of the American Protestant evangelical movement for at least 150 years. Both at the scholarly and popular level there are significant numbers of confessing Christians who wish to identify themselves as evangelicals who have embraced the seminal thesis of Kant's and Schleiermacher's thought. What Protestant Liberal theologians embraced in the nineteenth century—which culminated in Charles Sheldon's asking, "What would Jesus do?"—evangelicals popularized in the late twentieth century. Rather than ask, Who *is* Jesus? What has he done, what is he doing, and what will he do as a result of who he *is*?, the primary concern among Protestant Liberals and many alleged evangelicals is on doing what Jesus did. Jesus' uniqueness has been jettisoned. What Auguste Sabatier and Charles Augustus Briggs embraced in the late nineteenth century regarding the supremacy of feelings over beliefs, Shane Claiborne, Donald Miller, and a host of "emerging" church followers perpetuate today.[26] It is one thing to confess that Christianity

25. Hoffecker, "Enlightenments and Awakenings," in *Revolutions in Worldview*, 263–64, reveals the religious character of Kant's upbringing: "Kant's mother summarized their religious environment by the following entry in the family Bible: 'In the year 1724, on Saturday the 22nd of April at 5:00 in the morning, my son Immanuel was born into the world and on the 23rd received holy baptism. . . . May God preserve him in His covenant of grace unto his blessed end, for Jesus Christ's sake, Amen.' The sad reality was that Kant, apparently "coached to exhibit deep religious feelings" at the school to which he was sent while a young boy, testified to the "fear and trembling that overtook him whenever he recalled those days of youthful slavery and that he could never engage in prayer or hymn singing for the remainder of his life" (264).

26. Sabatier, *Outlines of a Philosophy of Religion*, 311–12, writes: "Truths of the religious and moral order are known by a subjective act of what Pascal calls *the heart*. Science can know nothing about them, for they are not in its order." Shane Claiborne,

cannot be reduced to thoughts or doctrines. All the great theologians throughout the history of the Christian church have affirmed that the Christian faith cannot be reduced simply to doctrines and thoughts. It is intellectually vacuous, however, to write a book attempting to explain what one believes and to convince others of its truthfulness, all the while affirming that doctrines are not very compelling or that the Christian faith, or spirituality, cannot be explained.

What we have in these examples is the complete bifurcation of religious faith from reason, the subjective from the objective, and being from doing. They are the manifestation of Kant's and Schleiermacher's thought. The system of thought that believes that the religious consciousness of the individual is the proper subject of theology, substitutes the person for God; anthropology replaces theology. Everything that biblical Christianity teaches that God has done, is doing, and will do is turned on its head and has been regarded as what humans must do in the reconceptualized Christianity of Schleiermacher. It is the latter that has been significantly embraced by American evangelicals. It is not surprising, then, that the Social Gospel that places emphasis on what humans do to bring God's kingdom has also become increasingly popular in American evangelical circles. What is denied in Kant's and Schleiermacher's system of thought is the notion that there is a realm of reality that must be interpreted in a particular way and that its interpretation can be known by humans. As a result, feelings and actions reign supreme. It is why sincerity is often regarded as the ultimate test for truth, and why many confessing Christians and churches are obsessed with what they alone must do in order to bring the kingdom of God.

How then does this pattern of thought manifest itself with respect to the issue of the integration of faith and learning? Rather than recognizing that God created all things as already integrated, and therefore recognizing that the aim of human thinking is to discern the integration that God created, it falls right in line with Kantian strains of thought and

---

The Irresistible Revolution, 28, writes: "The things that transform us, especially us 'postmoderns,' are people and experiences. Political ideologies and religious doctrines just aren't very compelling, even if they're true." Donald Miller, *Blue Like Jazz*, 57, writes: "I don't think you can explain how Christian faith works either. It is a mystery. And I love this about Christian spirituality. It cannot be explained, and yet it is beautiful and true. It is something you feel and comes from the soul." For a critique of the Emergent church movement, and its more popular practitioners, see Carson, *Becoming Conversant with the Emerging Church*.

frames integration as something humans must do. When this is how confessing Christians think about the matter of integration they have little hope of presenting a Christian view of reality or any subject within it, because in principle they have already denied perhaps the most seminal thought that directs all Christian thinking—that God exists and that he is the source of and controlling presence in all reality.

CONCLUSION

If schools and parents are to provide a distinctly Christian education, they must recognize not only these historical currents—along with this fundamental problem that exists today in the areas of human thought, learning, and knowledge in relation to Christianity—but also that much of what characterizes the thinking and work of those identifying themselves as Christians is, in important ways, unbiblical. The solution is not to try to recapture a bygone era but to bring every thought captive to the obedience of Christ, that is, to recognize that Jesus is Lord over all things, all the time. The solution is to recognize that every human knowledge claim is inherently theological, because God is the creator of all reality and no single reality can be rightly understood unless it is understood in relation to God and brought into service to him. The Bible does not teach that there is a fact/value divide, although it does reveal that such a divide exists in the thinking of people who are rebelling against Christ's lordship. Neither is there a dissolving of these realities into one so that every knowledge claim is automatically rendered true, just, and good, all the while demonstrating contradiction to other claims that are rendered equally true, just, and good. The creator is not dissolved into his creation, nor disconnected from it; he is distinct from it, or distinguishable from it, precisely because he is the personal creator Lord who upholds it, interprets it, and is present in it. He therefore can be experienced in it and will judge all those who render knowledge claims in it and about it, because those claims are ultimately about him.

3

Man and the Integrated Universe

*Thoughtful people, even many who are not Christians, have become im-
pressed with the shortcomings of our secularized schools. We have provided
technical education, which may make the youth of our country better able
to make use of the advances of natural science; but natural science, with its
command over the physical world, is not all that there is in human life. There
are also moral interests of mankind, and without cultivation of these moral
interests a technically trained man is only given more power to do harm.
By this purely secular, nonmoral, and nonreligious training we produce not
a real human being but a horrible Frankenstein, and we are beginning to
shrink back from the product of our own hands.*[1]

—J. Gresham Machen

IN MUCH OF WHAT passes for Christian schooling today the prevailing paradigm for understanding the relationship between faith and
learning is based on an "integrative" approach. In other words, it is
thought that one of the major functions of the Christian educator is to
integrate the Christian faith (i.e., biblical principles) with the truth of a
given academic discipline.[2] Defining what is meant by "integration" and

---

1. Machen, "The Necessity of the Christian School," 167–168. It is important to note
that neither Machen nor the Old Princeton tradition advocated a view that there actually could be "secular" or "nonmoral" education. Rather, here Machen affirms what
the advocates of this kind of education think of their education. In truth, according to
Machen and the Old Princetonians, all education is moral. See Helseth, *"Right Reason"
and the Princeton Mind.*

2. While we speak of Christian education in general at certain points, the main
target of our book is Christian schooling. And, of course, what we are asserting has
important implications for homeschoolers.

the "truth of a given academic discipline" was one of the major goals of chapter 1. Chapter 2, then, sought to show how the presuppositions underlying the integration paradigm have, historically, had more in common with secular humanistic philosophy than biblical Christianity. The current chapter, in turn, seeks to show how the integration paradigm fails to rightly understand the reality of the world as presented in Scripture. Stated differently, chapter 3 seeks to understand some of what Scripture teaches about the relationship between faith and learning and the implications that this has for the integration paradigm.

INTEGRATED REALITY: GOD CREATED ALL THINGS

Scripture begins with a simple and yet profound statement: "In the beginning, God created the heavens and the earth."[3] The phrase "heavens and the earth" is a summary way of referring to everything that exists other than God himself. This is where the concept of *creatio ex nihilo*— creation out of nothing—or absolute creation comes from.[4] Prior to God's creating work, nothing existed except God. God did not create the universe and its inhabitants out of materials that already existed (this is known as secondary creation); instead, God created the raw materials themselves and shaped them into the universe as man now knows it. This is drastically different from every form of human creativity. Human beings are not capable of absolute creation; they are only capable of relative (or secondary) creation—creating out of preexisting materials. For example, a sculptor does not first create the granite that he is going to shape into the bust of a great political leader. No, he chooses the granite, which exists apart from his own creative effort, and then shapes the preexisting block into his creation.[5]

Not only does God's *ability to create* something out of nothing differ from human creativity, but God's *mode of creating* also differs from man's modes of creating. Scripture makes it clear that God created by

3. Gen 1:1, ESV.

4. Bavinck, *In the Beginning*; Collins, *Genesis 1–4*, 50; Kelly, *Creation and Change*; Van Groningen, *From Creation to Consummation*, 5–49; Young, *Studies in Genesis One*; Wenham, *Genesis 1–15*. These do not agree on every point, but we have found them all to be of immense help. Some of their work will require the reader to know Hebrew, but the non-original language reader can still benefit.

5. This premise on an epistemological level is the basis for Anselm's (1033–1109) famous "Ontological Argument." Cf. Anselm, *Proslogion*, 7–9; Rauhut, *Ultimate Questions*, 191–196.

speaking—by the power and authority of his voice. The phrase "God said" (or some variant) occurs no less than nine times in the opening chapter of Genesis.[6] The Apostle John begins his Gospel by stating that, "In the beginning was the Word, and the Word was with God, and the Word was God. He was in the beginning with God. *All things were made through him, and without him was not any thing made that was made.*"[7] The fact that God creates by speech means that the creating work of God is a communicative act on God's part and that the universe and everything in it are, indeed, words of God. Martin Luther, in his exegetical notes on Genesis 1, writes,

> God calls into existence the things which do not exist (Rom 4:17) . . . He speaks true and existent realities. Accordingly, that which among us has the sound of a word is a reality with God. Thus sun, moon, heaven, earth, Peter, Paul, I, you, etc.—we are all words of God, in fact only one single syllable or letter by comparison with the entire creation. We, too, speak, but only according to the rules of language; that is, we assign names to objects which have already been created. But the divine rule of language is different, namely: when He says: "Sun, shine," the sun is there at once and shines. Thus the words of God are realities, not bare words.[8]

One may take this further and rightly conclude that the entire creating work of God—both *what* is created and *how* it is created—is an act of God revealing himself. Paul makes this clear in Romans 1 when he writes, "For what can be known about God is plain to them, because God has shown it to them. For his invisible attributes, namely, his eternal power and divine nature, have been clearly perceived, ever since the creation of the world, in the things that have been made. So they are without excuse."[9] In other words, the entire creation is a manifestation of God's power and authority, and thereby his presence; everything that exists reveals God in some way or another, because the entire creation exists by and for God.[10] Thus, the creation is a whole and coherent entity

---

6. Gen 1:3, 6, 9, 11, 14, 20, 22, 24, 26, 28; also God's "calling" of entities into existence and his "calling" them into order.

7. John 1:1–3, ESV, emphasis added.

8. *Luther's Works*. Vol. 1, *Lectures on Genesis: Chapters 1–5*, 21–22.

9. Rom 1:19–20, ESV.

10. Col 1:16–17. See Frame, *The Doctrine of the Knowledge of God*, 15–18; Frame, *The Doctrine of God*, 102; Frame, *The Doctrine of the Word of God*, 50–68.

rather than a fragmented and disjointed nonentity (or chaos); the entire universe functions together to reveal God.[11] For this reason the universe can be rightly considered a created *order*, or a created *system*.

INTEGRATED REALITY: GOD ORDERED ALL THINGS

The text of Genesis moves from God revealing himself in and through absolute creation (Gen 1:1) to God revealing himself in and through the organization of the creation (Gen 1:2–31).[12] That is, Genesis 1:2–31 show God building certain patterns, relationships, and orders into the creation. This may be seen in a brief examination of the work of God on each of the seven days of the creating week that form the story line.[13]

11. The Hebrew terms translated as "formless" and "void" should likely be understood to be telling us that the earth was in an uninhabitable condition, that is, probably not best described as chaotic. The latter term can carry connotations that the Hebrew terms do not necessarily imply and that their use elsewhere in the Old Testament denies. That God did not create the world to be uninhabited can be seen in Isa 45:18, with the same Hebrew term (*tohu*) found in Gen. 1:2 there translated as "empty" or "void." See Young, *Studies in Genesis One*, 12–13; Collins, *Genesis 1–4*, 54; contra Bruce Waltke on the latter's understanding of what is communicated regarding "formless" and "void."

12. Or "forming." The exact relationship between the first two verses of Genesis and the relationship of verse one to the rest of the chapter are hotly debated. One of the things God is driving us toward in the ambiguity is the obvious necessity to rely upon the rest of his written word to give us aid in our understanding of these verses. That is, we must rely upon what is called "the analogy of Scripture." The basic question regarding the relationship of Gen 1:1 to 1:2, and indeed the rest of the chapter, is whether verse 1 is a dependent or an independent clause. Without giving a detailed explanation, we affirm that it is an independent clause that must be understood to communicate absolute creation or creation *ex nihilo* (out of nothing). See Isa 45:18; 46:10–11; John 1:1–4; Col 1:16–17; Heb 11:3. Young, *Studies in Genesis One*, 1–14; Collins, *Genesis 1–4*, 50–55. It also highlights the very character of theological or doctrinal work: it uses words to communicate concepts, and thus highlights the primacy of concepts, not merely particular words. In other words, by the very nature of the text we have an emphasis on human *thinking* that is central to who we are and what God has for us to do.

13. Collins, *Genesis 1–4*, 42–44, highlights the importance of the verb that begins verse 3 as the one that carries the story line forward, and he further identifies the whole passage from 1:1—2:3 as "exalted prose narrative." In other words, those who allow the majestic character of the literary style to lead them to identify the text as poetic or "mythical," and who contend that the events described do not actually correspond to what we experience as creatures bound by time and space, are exercising their will over and against the text. Collins believes 1:1–2 should be regarded together with verse 3 as beginning the main story line. Whether one sides with Collins, or Young et al. that 1:1 stands alone and 2–31 should be grouped together, one thing is clear: the grammar provides no clarity regarding *how much time, as we humans experience it, there was between the condition of verse 2 and God's speaking mentioned in verse 3.*

On the first creating day, God separates light from darkness and, in doing so, establishes a specific relationship between light and darkness, as well as a pattern of transitions between light and darkness that marks what human beings know as day and night and that govern practically all of human life in some way, shape, or form.[14] On the second creating day, God separates the waters above from the waters below; that is, he separates the clouds—atmospheric water—from the water on the earth's surface. By doing so, God establishes a specific relationship between clouds and water on the earth's surface, a relationship that orders the cycles of evaporation and rain that are integral to all life on earth.[15] On the third creating day, God gathers together the waters on the earth into seas, forming dry land and effectively establishing the basis for the complex ecosystems that he begins on the third creating day and continues on the fifth and sixth creating days.[16] God's work on the fourth creating day orders the sun, moons, and stars, establishing specific relationships between them that have been the object of man's astronomical studies.[17] The fifth and sixth creating days bring animal life to the creation, which complete the complex ecosystems that were begun on the third creating day.[18] The sixth creating day also brings the crowning achievement of God's creating work—mankind, which, unlike all the other living organisms in the creation, is created in the image of God.

In the creation of man, God's organizing work in creation is even more apparent. Genesis 2:7 states that "the LORD God *formed the man of the dust from the ground* and breathed into his nostrils the breath of life, and the man became a living creature."[19] The manner of man's creation is reiterated in the curse he incurs after the entrance of sin into the created order: "By the sweat of your face you shall eat bread, till you return to the ground, for out of it you were taken; for you are dust, and to dust you shall return."[20] The implication is that the material of which man is made is not unique to him (a fact that is supported by modern

14. Gen 1:3–5.
15. Gen 1:6–8.
16. Gen 1:9–13.
17. Gen 1:14–19.
18. Gen 1:20–25.
19. ESV, emphasis added.
20. Gen 3:19.

science);[21] instead, it is what God has determined we would be and do as creatures *created in his image* and placed within the already integrated creation that comprises our uniqueness.[22]

Furthermore, with the creation of man in God's image, a hierarchy within creation is established. Man is given the responsibility to rule over the creation, to not only nurture and grow life on earth, but to subdue all life on earth, to use it for his benefit and beauty unto the glory of God.[23] Finally, on the seventh day in the creating week, God rests and, by doing so, establishes a cycle of work and rest that is necessary for life. Indeed, the human concept of a week, in which one differentiates between work and rest, is itself built into the creation, built into the very fabric of human existence, by God's work of organizing the creation in Genesis 1:2–31.

Thus, the organizing work of God recorded in Genesis 1:2–31 established specific relationships between created entities in the universe.[24] These relationships are comprised of specific orders, patterns, hierarchies, and the like, which cause the universe to function in specific ways (such as the aforementioned cycle of evaporation and rain that marks the relationship between clouds and water covering the earth), and so God is determining how the relationships will function in and among themselves. In other words, *God integrated the universe and everything within it.*[25] That is, Genesis 1:2–31 presents *God* as the unifying (integrating) power and presence in the universe; he holds all things together.[26] All truth is of and from God, because God himself is truth, and so all truth is related in and through God.[27]

Furthermore, because all truth is a revelation of the God who created and integrated the universe, all true knowledge is knowledge of

21. Talero and Talero, *Foundations in Microbiology*, 26–57.

22. Thought, feeling, and action are essential to what it means for man to be made in the image of God in Gen 1:26; see the section below titled "Man and the Integrated Reality" for a more detailed explanation.

23. Gen 1:28–30.

24. "Created entities" refers to all created elements and organisms in all of their arrangements, everything from oxygen to hydrogen, from water to water lilies, from locusts to dogs to man.

25. See chapter 1 for the definition of "integration."

26. Col 1:16–17.

27. Deut 32:4; Jer 10:10; Ps 119:160; John 1:14; 14:6; 17:3; Rom 3:4; Eph 1:13; 1 John 5:20.

God, and all true learning is learning about God. Because the creation is itself a revelation of God, studying and learning about the creation is ultimately studying and learning about God—and, therefore, all human learning has God as its ultimate object. It is for this reason that systematic theology was, for much of church history, considered the Queen of the Sciences (here *science* is used in its most basic form to refer to knowledge). In the words of B.B. Warfield, "It is thus as true of science as it is of creatures, that in Him they all live and move and have their being. The science of Him and His relations is the necessary ground of all science. All speculation takes us back to Him; all inquiry presupposes Him . . . It is only in theology, therefore, that the other sciences find their completion."[28] Because systematic theology has God, the creator and integrator of all things, as the object of its study, systematic theology provides the right framework[29] for understanding all life and every human endeavor. This does not mean that the Christian ought not to engage in biology, physics, and chemistry, or in studies of literature, language, and history. On the contrary, these disciplines are highly important, for all academic disciplines seek to better understand the universe that God created (albeit from different perspectives, but because of the vastness of God and his creation, different perspectives are exactly what is needed to come to a better understanding of God and his creation). Therefore the Christian ought to engage in such studies. However, the position of systematic theology as the Queen of the Sciences means that advancements in all academic disciplines will not be rightly understood apart from a right understanding of God, which is the goal of systematic theology.[30] In the words of John M. Frame, "[I]n knowing our world, we know God. Because God is the supreme authority, the author of all criteria by which we make judgments or come to conclusions, we know Him more certainly than we know any other fact about the world."[31] And again, Frame writes,

> Knowing God involves knowing His world for several reasons.
> (1) Just as knowing God's authority involves knowing His law, so

28. Warfield, "The Idea of Systematic Theology," 71.

29. By "framework" we mean an organizing principle or set of principles; a paradigm, a worldview.

30. For further study, see Warfield, "The Idea of Systematic Theology," 49–87; Warfield, "The Right of Systematic Theology," 219–279.

31. Frame, *The Doctrine of the Knowledge of God*, 20.

knowing God's control involves knowing His "mighty works," that is, His works of creation, providence, and redemption. The world itself is a mighty work of God, and the whole course of nature and history comes under that category as well. (2) Furthermore, we know God by means of the world. All of God's revelation comes through creaturely means, whether events, prophets, Scripture, or merely the human eye or ear. Thus we cannot know anything about God without knowing something about the world at the same time. Also, (3) God wants His people to apply His Word to their own situations, and this implies that He wants them to understand their own situations. We have a warrant for studying the world. To know God obediently, then, we must know something about the world as well. The converse is also true. We cannot know the world without knowing God. As we have seen, God is "clearly seen" in the creation.[32]

To claim that knowing God necessitates knowing the world and vice versa is to acknowledge that all truth is interrelated—or integrated—by, in, through, and for God. Such is Paul's point in Colossians when he says, "For *by him all things were created*, in heaven and on earth, visible and invisible, whether thrones or dominions or rulers or authorities—*all things were created through him and for him*. And he is before all things, and *in him all things hold together*."[33] In the words of E. B. Pusey,

All things must speak of God, refer to God, or they are atheistic. History, without God, is a chaos without design, or end, or aim. Political Economy, without God, would be a selfish teaching about the acquisition of wealth, making the larger portion of mankind animate machines for its production; Physics, without God, would be but a dull inquiry into certain meaningless phenomena; Ethics, without God, would be a varying rule, without principle, or substance, or centre, or regulating hand; Metaphysics, without God, would make man his own temporary god, to be resolved, after his brief hour here, into the nothingness out of which he proceeded.[34]

There are three serious implications for the current discussion on education that must be stated at this point. The first is that God's creation is an integrated and coherent reality; that all truth is of and from God.

32. Ibid., 64.

33. Col 1:16–17, ESV, emphasis added.

34. Pusey, "Collegiate and Professorial Teaching and Discipline," 215–216. Cited in Warfield, "The Idea of Systematic Theology," 70–71.

The second is that the job of the Christian educator is not to integrate faith and knowledge (or faith and learning), for the two are already integrated in and by God. To presume that we must is not simply folly but arrogance. The third is that any philosophy of education that assumes a rift between faith and knowledge—such as the integrative paradigm in much of what passes for Christian schooling today—is not based on the witness of Scripture.

MAN AND THE INTEGRATED REALITY

Because God is the source of all truth, and all truth is a revelation of God, it follows that all truth is religious and (therefore) moral in nature, for the God whom it reveals and in whom it finds its source is a moral being (that is, he is holy, righteous, and good).[35] Those who attempt to draw a distinction between religious knowledge and secular knowledge (or between moral and non-moral knowledge) fail to understand the universe rightly: as a coherent and integrated system whose source and maintenance is in the living God who is himself the source of all truth and knowledge. Moreover, the crowning work of God's creating activity—mankind—was created to live within and learn about the morality revealed by God in the created order. Thus, man is a moral being, too. Hence, education that attempts to be non-moral (or secular) succeeds only in harming the learner and producing what J. Gresham Machen called "a horrible Frankenstein."[36]

A brief exposition of the creation of mankind will help clarify this point. It was not until God created man in his own image and gave him dominion over the rest of the creation that God stepped back, looked at the works of his hands, and declared that "it was very good."[37] Until Genesis 1:26 (the creation of man), God looked at the creation and "saw that it was good,"[38] but after the creation of man it was "very good." Douglas Kelly writes, "In Genesis 1:26 there is a notable shift in lan-

35. Deut 25:1; Ps 36:6; Amos 3:2; Matt 5:48; Mark 10:18; Luke 18:19; Eph 4:23–24; 1 John 3:7.

36. Machen, "The Necessity of the Christian School," 168. See the quote at the beginning of this chapter and footnote one. If supposedly secular, nonmoral education was producing a "Frankenstein" as early as 1933, when Machen wrote this address, one wonders what allegedly secular, nonmoral education is producing today.

37. Gen 1:31, NAS.

38. Gen 1:4, 10, 12, 18, 21, 25, NAS.

guage, indicating the highest stage in all the week's creative activity."[39] Man alone is created in the image of God. Whereas all other plant and animal life is created "according to their own kinds,"[40] man is created according to God's own kind.[41] That is, man is patterned after God. As Kelly states,

> The content of "the image or likeness of God" could probably safely be summed up in the post-biblical term, "personal." That is, because he is in the image of God, man is personal or has personality. The contemporary usage of "person" as synonymous with "individual" and "personality" with a collection of particular "traits" does not fully express the Biblical meaning of the concept of "image of God" nor the Christian reflection of it in the development of "personal terminology [i.e. in the Trinity]…It may be sufficient to note here that the "likeness or image" of God (or the term "personal") bears the idea of mind, will, affections, and especially *relationship* with other similar persons. That is to say, a single person does not exist without other persons to give him or her meaning. That is the concept that may be hinted at by the plural usage of Genesis 1:26, 'Let us make', and 'our.'[42]

C. John Collins provides a helpful summary regarding how we should think of humans as created in God's image.[43] Drawing upon the features of Genesis 1:26–28, the rest of Scripture, and the history of Christian theology, Collins names three basic options regarding this matter: the *resemblance, representative,* and *relational* views. The *resemblance* view stresses some aspect of our being, such as rationality, and identifies "image of God" primarily, although not exclusively, in the category of ontology or metaphysics. The *representative* and *relational* views primarily, although not exclusively, stress our functions. The *rep-*

---

39. Kelly, *Creation and Change*, 216; Collins, *Genesis 1–4*, 72, notes that the verb *created* appears three times in Gen 1:27 but only once in the Hebrew verb form that carries the story line forward and that is used through Genesis 1:3–31. Thus, the text is alerting the reader to dwell on the reality of God creating man, male and female, in his image.

40. Gen 1:11, 12, 21, 24, 25.

41. Gen 1:26.

42. Kelly, *Creation and Change*, 219–20, emphasis original.

43. Collins, *Genesis 1–4*, 61–67. There is a legitimate debate regarding the difference between being created *in* or *according to* the image of God versus being *the* image of God. However, this debate does not impinge upon our two fundamental assertions: 1) that humans possess uniqueness to the other creatures in vitally important ways, and 2) that humans were and still are integrated to God and the rest of creation.

resentative view highlights our representing God in our work of having dominion over the creatures and subduing the earth, while the *relational* view highlights our personal relationship first to God and then each other, with the latter focused on the marriage of the man and the woman. We concur with Collins that one makes a critical mistake if one plays these off against each other. The text is teaching that none of these is to be regarded as independent of the others but that, in fact, they mutually define each other. Ultimately, it reveals that all we *are* as humans and all that we are to *do* was integrated by God at creation; we exist in an integrated condition with God and creation because of what God did. Although sin damaged this integrated condition, it did not destroy or obliterate it, as Genesis 3, and indeed the rest of Scripture, reveals.

In Genesis 1:26–31 man's personality (i.e., his being created in the image of God) is expressly connected with having dominion over the created order and living harmoniously with it and other human beings (expressed ideally by the marriage covenant in Genesis 2:24–25). So then, the fact that man is created in the image of God means that man was created to relate with the world around him by expressing dominion over the creation, in harmony with other human beings, as representatives of God. Gerard Van Groningen summarizes by stating,

> God established a vital, binding relationship between himself and mankind when he created Adam in his image and likeness. This relationship is an essential aspect of God's covenant. The foundational idea of covenant is bond. God bound himself to mankind as he bound mankind to himself. It was a bond of life and love. It was a bond that was to be expressed in a variety of ways. If the bond functioned as it was intended, that is, as an *intimate fellowship with God* and *fellow men* and an obedient, devoted service with reference to *the whole creation*, mankind would be blessed.[44]

In order to fulfill these three responsibilities man would have to "continue in fellowship with the sovereign Creator and Lord. Man was to live under the express command of God (Gen 2:16–17) and so doing remain within the will of the sovereign Lord."[45] In fact, man's threefold responsibility can be summarized as, "obey God." Hence, when Jesus is

---

44. Van Groningen, *Messianic Revelation in the Old Testament*, 103, emphasis added.

45. Ibid., 104.

asked by the Pharisees, "Teacher, which is the great commandment in the Law," Jesus responds by saying, "You shall love the Lord your God with all your heart and with all your soul and with all your mind. This is the great and first commandment."[46] In short, man was created to know God, to live in harmony with God by remaining obedient to God's revealed moral standard. This is the picture given in Genesis 2 and 3, in which God walks in the garden with man, teaches man his will directly, and provides for all of man's needs.[47] In order to know God and live in harmony with him, man would have to properly exercise his capacities to think, act, and feel; that is, properly express his personality as the only being created in the image of God. For it is through these capacities to think, act, and feel that man understands and interacts with the world around him, and thereby relates to God.

That man would have to properly exercise his capacities to think, act, and feel in order to properly relate with God is seen more clearly in the Greek word for repentance, *metanoia*, which means "a change in mind or thinking." Because the Bible teaches that humans are a unified whole of body and soul, thinking (or mind) is intimately and inseparably united to action and feeling. Biblical repentance, then, includes all of man's being—everything that he is and does as he cares for creation, interacts with other human beings, and fellowships with God.

An example of this can be seen in the child who disobeys his parents' command not to play in the woods because in it there is much poison ivy. He disobeys and gets the poison ivy on his skin. He becomes physically miserable because of the itching and regrets having disobeyed. His repentance consists of coming to understand that the command was meant for his good, not for stifling his pleasure; of being sorrowful for the consequences of his disobedience; of confessing his sin and his sorrow for it to his parents; and, ultimately, of agreeing with God's word that obedience to his parents is good and that rebelling against them is akin to rebelling against God. Repentance consists of knowing such things, agreeing that God's word concerning his relationship to his parents is good, and endeavoring to obey God's word in his relationship to

---

46. Matt 22:36–38, ESV. The fact that Jesus summarized the Ten Commandments, and indeed all "the Law and the Prophets," in one command is an example of and warrant for systematic theology.

47. Gen 3:8; Gen 2:15, 16–17, 18–25.

his parents. Though it all can be characterized as a "change of mind," it is addressing the whole person—thoughts, feelings and actions.

Similarly, man's understanding of God directs him to do (or not do) certain things and causes him to feel certain emotions about God. This is the point of Proverbs 1:7, which states, "The fear of the Lord is the beginning of knowledge. . . ."[48] The fear of God spoken of in the first chapter of Proverbs is an informed fear, that is, a fear based on a right understanding of God's holiness and righteousness and man's lack thereof. This knowledge of God's perfection and man's imperfection causes fear, and this fear will direct a man to live a life that is obedient to the will of God (the rest of the book of Proverbs outlines what qualities and characteristics mark a life that is obedient to the will of God). Thus, this fear is perhaps best described as reverence leading to repentance, which in turn leads to knowledge of the truth (2 Tim 2:25).[49] The goal, then, of all of our intellectual endeavors—our learning—is to better understand the God who created us that we may live in obedience to him.

SO WHAT?

Knowing God and living in obedience to him is the goal of all human learning, and as such, all human learning is inherently religious and moral in nature. There is no such thing as a divide between religious and secular knowledge or between moral and amoral knowledge. Indeed, strictly speaking there is no such thing as secular or amoral knowledge, except in the thinking of people who think unbiblically. All truth is God's truth. All truth reveals the God who created and integrated all things. Therefore, all truth is religious and moral. While sin has adversely affected man's knowledge of God and his ability to live in obedience to him, it has not excused man from his obligation to know God and live a life of obedience to him.[50] In order to know God and live obediently to him, man must exercise dominion over the created order and love fellow human beings; it requires man to know and care for the world around him, for knowledge of the Creator and knowledge of the creation are

48. ESV.

49. Certainly, Paul is addressing the specific context of correcting falsehoods in others, but the point is that repentance leads to knowledge of truth; how exactly we are brought to that repentance does not determine what characterizes the relationship between repentance and truth.

50. This will be taken up in the following chapter, "The Noetic Effects of Sin."

inseparably related, because the creation is a revelation of the one who created it. Furthermore, the creation exists in a specific, God-ordained, order; he has organized the creation so as to function in particular ways, and he upholds and sustains this organization. That is, God created and integrated the world, and the way in which he integrated the world is further revelation of him. God is the integrating power and presence; he is that which holds all things together; everything exists by him, through him, and for him. This is the point of Colossians 1:16–17, which states, "For by him all things were created, in heaven and on earth, visible and invisible, whether thrones or dominions or rulers or authorities—all things were created through him and for him. And he is before all things, and in him all things hold together."[51]

The goal of Christian education, therefore, is not to integrate the religious knowledge found in Scripture with the knowledge found in putatively secular textbooks. Whatever truth may be found in such textbooks can only be considered as such precisely because it conforms to creation as it is, on account of God having created it that way. The truth found in Scripture is already in harmony with whatever truth may be in the textbooks. Any seeming disagreements can only be the result of errors in the textbooks, or errors in understanding the textbooks, or errors in understanding Scripture, or the failure to rightly understand how certain truths relate to one another (i.e., how they are integrated). The goal of Christian education is to seek to understand the integrated world that God has created; to know God better by knowing him as he has expressed himself in all truth, in all academic disciplines; to know God better by understanding how science, literature, history, art, etc., relate to one another (i.e., how they are integrated), for their integration is created and sustained by God himself, and as such, is a revelation of God. Simply put, the goal of Christian education is to understand the relationship between all truth (i.e. the points of integration) and the subsequent implications for human thought, action, and feeling.

To assume a rift between religious and secular (or moral and amoral) knowledge is entirely unbiblical. To operate, even, with these two distinct epistemological categories is ultimately unbiblical. As we sought to make clear in chapter 2, such an assumption is based on the philosophical presuppositions of modernism and postmodernism and (as this chapter has attempted to demonstrate) *not* Scripture. Furthermore,

51. ESV.

such an assumption thinks too highly of man. Who is man that he could manipulate reality itself—first in disintegrating truth and creating two distinct categories for truth, and secondly in integrating religious and secular knowledge? But this is precisely what the integration paradigm in Christian schooling assumes: that all truth was at one point integrated and coherent but that man disintegrated them, and now man—more specifically Christian schools—must reintegrate them. While many in Christian education will quickly deny that they need to do what God has already done, they too often operate as if they need and/or ought to do what God has already done. Indeed, one of the major problems with the integrative paradigm is that many of the people using it and/or discussing it do not truly understand its underlying presuppositions.[52]

The integration framework is inherently misguided. It focuses on what man is able to do and not what God has already done. Because worldview integration was one of the founding principles of the Christian school movement that started in the mid-twentieth century, much of what passes for Christian schooling today has the same problem: it is focused on that which man is able to measure, manipulate, manufacture, and manage rather than what God has already done. As a result, Christian schools often look and feel very similar to non-Christian public and private schools; the ways in which the schools are structured and operate are essentially the same.

The focus on what man is able to do often leads Christian schools to talk a lot about changes, while never actually effecting any substantive change. For example, a Christian school may spend a great deal of time and resources to discuss the nature of an integrated curriculum, but in the end the curriculum will remain relatively unchanged. Or a Christian school may spend a great deal of time and energy in discussing the "unique design" of each individual student and the implications it has for education (both for the teacher and for the student), but in the end, very little of what is discussed has any bearing on the classroom. Still another Christian school may focus on professional development or best practices and yet, ultimately, these become nothing more than hoops for teachers to jump through—another box to check off that has no significant effect on what happens in the classroom. Thus, the programs that are intended to improve Christian schooling—to make it more Christ-

---

52. Chapter 2 seeks to uncover the underlying presuppositions of the integration paradigm.

centered and biblically faithful—fail because they are based on flawed presuppositions from the start. One writer and educator calls these types of programs "silver bullet solutions" because teachers and administrators expect them to be a cure-all, but the reality is that "systemic change is not something you can just photocopy and cheer on."[53]

When Christian educators lose a biblical focus—when they spend the majority of their time and energy focusing on their spheres of influence and what they are able to measure, manipulate, manufacture, and manage rather than on what God has already done, is doing, and will do, as well as how he does it—they fail to be faithful to what Scripture would have them do. That which we are actually able to measure, manipulate, manufacture, and manage on our own is small and insignificant; when this is the focus Christian schooling, the results are not what they could be. Christian education does not need another program to implement, nor another meeting, committee, or in-service to discuss change; it does not need a better model and/or method of integration. As simple as it may sound, Christian educators need to rightly understand God. We need to rightly understand what God, as Creator-King, has done, is doing, and will do—and the implications this has for us all. In the words of David Wells, "The fundamental problem in the evangelical world today is not inadequate technique, [or] insufficient organization . . . The fundamental problem in the evangelical world today is that God rests inconsequentially upon the Church. His truth is too distant, his grace is too ordinary, his judgment is too benign, his gospel is too easy, and his Christ is too common."[54] What plagues many evangelical churches plagues many of the schools affiliated with them, not to mention many of the educators going to those churches. Christian education needs systemic change, a revolution, a reformation that will reorient it toward the truth concerning the doctrine of God, as the covenant Creator Lord, so that it will stop spending so much time focusing on the finite and fallen abilities of humans.

---

53. Stover, "Reform School," 15–18. Quoted in Hess, *Education Unbound*, 6.
54. Wells, *God in the Wasteland*, 30.

4

The Noetic Effects of Sin

Calvin's doctrine of the noetic [pertaining to the mind] effects of sin and their removal by the "testimony of the Spirit," that is to say, by what we call "regeneration," must not be taken as a doctrine of the unknowableness of God. On the contrary it is a doctrine of the knowableness of God, and supplies only an account of why men in the present condition fail to know Him, and an exposition of how and in what conditions the knowableness of God may manifest itself in man as now constituted in an actually known God. When the Spirit of God enters the heart with recreative power, he says, then even sinful man, his blurred eyes opened, may see God, not merely that there is a God, but what kind of being God is. [1]

—B. B. WARFIELD

THE PREVIOUS CHAPTER EMPHASIZED that the universe and everything in it exists and functions within certain God-ordained relationships and that as a result the universe exists and functions as a unified, coherent system; the universe is an integrated reality. This, in part, means that all true knowledge is integrated—it exists within certain God-determined relationships and functions as a coherent whole. Precisely because all knowledge is unified in the person and work of God all knowledge is ultimately knowledge of God. All knowledge, therefore, is religious and moral in nature; so-called secular knowledge does not exist. Thus, it is not necessary, nor is it possible, for man to reconcile secular knowledge with religious knowledge (which is typically referred to as "integration" within Christian schooling), for secular knowledge does not exist; all knowledge is moral and religious. At this point, it is

---

1. Warfield, "Calvin's Doctrine of God," 151.

important to note that sin has, indeed, affected man's ability to rightly know and discern this integrated reality but has not completely obliterated this ability, nor has it disintegrated reality, which would make a reintegration necessary. This chapter seeks to expound the doctrine of sin and its effect on man's ability to think and know, and how this relates to current methodological paradigms within Christian schooling.

TOTAL DEPRAVITY INTRODUCED

The doctrine of the Total Depravity of man has been disputed by different groups throughout the history of the church. Unfortunately, most of the disagreement over the doctrine of Total Depravity is caused by a lack of understanding on the part of those who dispute it. The totality of depravity does not mean that man is incapable of doing any good or that man is as corrupt as he possibly could be, so that each of us is the worst possible version of ourselves (as if we could not be any worse than we are now). The totality of depravity refers to the fact that there is no part of the human body, mind, or soul that is not corrupted by sin. In other words, everything that man is and does is affected by sin. For this reason, many Reformed scholars prefer the term *Radical Depravity* because it conveys that man is depraved at the "root" of his being (*radical* derives from the Latin word *radix*, meaning "root"). This, then, leads to the conclusion that man is incapable of doing anything that is *truly* good, that is, good in reference to God. Fred Zaspel, summarizing the thought of B. B. Warfield, acknowledges that "there is a distinction between social good and spiritual good. A sinner may well do what is 'good' in meeting the needs of his neighbor and of society."[2] But because of the corruption of sin—because sin affects everything that man is and does—it is impossible for man to do something good to or for God, something that meets God's standard of absolute perfection.[3] Paul, in Romans 3, summarizes the biblical teaching on the utter sinfulness of man by quoting from and expounding upon a number of Old Testament texts. He states,

> None is righteous, no not one; no one understands; no one seeks
> God. All have turned aside; together they have become worthless;

2. Zaspel, *The Theology of B. B. Warfield*, 403.

3. It is not within the scope of this book to present the doctrine of Total Depravity in full. For a more in-depth discussion on the topic, see Calvin, *The Institutes of the Christian Religion*, I.i–II.v; Dabney, *Lectures in Systematic Theology*, 321–332; Zaspel, *The Theology of B. B. Warfield*, 369–409.

no one does good, not even one. Their throat is an open grave; they use their tongues to deceive. The venom of asps is under their lips. Their mouth is full of curses and bitterness. Their feet are swift to shed blood; in their paths are ruin and misery, and the way of peace they have not known. There is no fear of God before their eyes.[4]

THE NOETIC EFFECTS OF SIN SUMMARIZED

One of the important aspects of the doctrine of Total Depravity is sin's effects on the human mind, or the noetic effects of sin.[5] Sin has corrupted and disordered man's mind to the extent that it is impossible for him, in his sinful and unregenerate state, to rightly recognize and discern the truth about God. In Romans 1, Paul affirms that certain attributes of God are clearly revealed in and through the creation itself but that man is unable to rightly respond to this revelation because his mind has been darkened, so much so that he suppresses revealed truth instead of accepting it.

> For the wrath of God is revealed from heaven against all ungodliness and unrighteousness of men, who by their unrighteousness *suppress the truth.* For what can be known about God is plain to them, because God has shown it to them. For his invisible attributes, namely, his eternal power and divine nature, *have been clearly perceived,* ever since the creation of the world, *in the things that have been made.* So they are without excuse. For *although they knew God, they did not honor him as God or give thanks to him,* but *they became futile in their thinking,* and their *foolish hearts were darkened.* Claiming to be wise, *they became fools,* and exchanged the glory of the immortal God for images resembling mortal man and birds and animals and creeping things.[6]

And again in Romans 8:6–8, "For to set the mind on the flesh is death, but to set the mind on the Spirit is life and peace. For *the mind that is set on the flesh is hostile to God, for it does not submit to God's law; indeed, it cannot.* Those who are in the flesh cannot please God."[7] And

---

4. Rom 3:10–18, ESV.

5. "Noetic" derives from the Greek word *noeō*, meaning "to perceive, understand, comprehend."

6. Rom 1:18–23, ESV, emphasis added.

7. ESV, emphasis added.

again in 1 Corinthians 2:14, "The natural person does not accept the things of the Spirit of God, for *they are folly to him, and he is not able to understand them because they are spiritually discerned.*"[8]

The revelation of God that is manifest in the creation can be referred to as "general revelation." It is general in that it is intended for all people, and it is general in that it is not detailed or specific; that is, it does not outline specific details about the person and work of God. General revelation confronts mankind with the fact that there is a God and points man in the right direction, so to speak, to discover who this God is and how he operates. Unfortunately, man's ability to rightly interpret and then, in turn, rightly respond to general revelation has been seriously hindered by sin. It is important at this point to note that the failure of general revelation to drive mankind to the living and true God is not rooted in the shortcomings of general revelation itself but in the noetic effects of sin. In the words of B. B. Warfield, "The failure of the general revelation of God to produce in men an adequate knowledge of Him is as universal as is the revelation itself. The explanation is to be found in the corruption of men's hearts by sin, by which not merely are they rendered incapable of reading off the revelation of God which is displayed in His works and deeds, but their very instinctive knowledge of God, embedded in their constitution as men, is dulled and almost obliterated."[9]

It is important to note that Warfield writes that it is "dulled and *almost* obliterated." While man's instinctive knowledge of God is seriously hindered because of sin's noetic effects, it is not gone altogether. Warfield argues that the fact that religion is not extinct but exists in so many varied forms is proof that the innate knowledge of God (*sensus deitatis*, or sense of deity) has not been completely destroyed in man. Furthermore, the wide variety of world religions proves that man is not able to rightly interpret or rightly respond to general revelation. But all is not lost; man is not hopelessly adrift in a sea of right and wrong ideas about God with no way of discerning which are which. That is, the human inability to rightly know and understand God does *not* mean that it is impossible for man to rightly know and understand God.

8. ESV, emphasis added.

9. Warfield, "Calvin and Calvinism," 43. Warfield was expositing Calvin's thought.

INABILITY VS. IMPOSSIBILITY

The quote from Warfield that begins this chapter states succinctly that the doctrine of the noetic effect of sin is not the "doctrine of the un-knowableness of God." In reality, the doctrine of the noetic effects of sin starts with the premise that Adam was created with knowledge of God, knew creation rightly, reasoned rightly about it, and acted righteously in it. This was the purpose for which God created Adam and Eve, but sin has corrupted man's ability to rightly know God. For man, in his sinful state, willingly suppresses the truth about God. This is the noetic effect of sin: the darkening of the human mind; choosing to be foolish concerning the things of God rather than wise. This does not mean that it is impossible for man in his sinful state to know anything rightly, as if only Christians can have real, true knowledge. On the contrary, man in his fallen state is able to know and discern a great deal about God and his creation. Obviously, man in his sinful state is able to rightly know certain truths about God; if this were not true, then how would a fallen man become a Christian? The point is that *apart from the work of the Holy Spirit*, man in his sinful state does not have a right understanding of God and his creation.[10] In other words, it is not impossible for man to attain a right knowledge of God; man is only unable to do this by himself. In the words of B. B. Warfield,

> Perhaps we may make this clear by an illustration drawn from the specific instance of "faith in God." Even as sinner, man cannot but believe in God: the very Devils believe—and tremble. But as sin-ner, man cannot have faith in God in the higher sense of humbly trusting in him. Precisely what sin has done to man is to destroy the root of this trust by altering the relation to God in which man stands . . . So long as he remains human he cannot escape the consciousness of dependence on God. But this consciousness no longer bears the same character as in the unfallen state. In the unfallen state consciousness of dependence on God took the "form" of glad and loving trust. By destroying the natural relation that exists between God and His creature and instituting a new relation—that proper to God and sinner—sin has introduced a new factor into the functioning of all human powers. The sinner instinctively and by his very nature, as he cannot help believing

10. The work of the Holy Spirit in guiding an individual into a right understanding of Scripture is often referred to as "illumination." For biblical support for the doctrine, see Isa 59:21; John 6:45; 16:13–14; 1 Cor 2:9–12.

in God, in the intellectual sense, so cannot possibly exercise faith in God in the fiducial [saving] sense. On the contrary faith in this sense has been transformed into its opposite—faith has passed into unfaith, trust into distrust. Faith now takes the "form" of fear and despair. The reestablishment of it in the "form" of loving trust cannot be the work for the sinner himself. It can result only from a radical change in the relation of the sinner to God, brought home to the sinner by that creative act of the Holy Ghost which we call the testimonium Spiritus Sancti [the testimony of the Holy Spirit].[11]

THE NOETIC EFFECTS OF REGENERATION

Precisely because sin effects a total change in man, a total change is needed if man is to be redeemed from sin. To state it differently, because every part of man is corrupted by sin, every part of him must be redeemed from sin. In John 3, Jesus tells Nicodemus that in order to enter the kingdom of God, one must be "born again"—born of the Spirit, not of the flesh.[12] Paul picks up on this same idea in 2 Corinthians when he states, "Therefore, if anyone is in Christ, he is a new creation."[13] This second birth, causing the redeemed individual to be considered a "new creation" is often called regeneration. "Regeneration is that act of God by which the principle of new life is implanted in man, and the governing disposition of the soul is made holy."[14] In other words, regeneration is God's work of resurrecting a deadened sinner so that he can begin the process of sanctification, or being made holy. That is, regeneration begins the process of reversing the effects of total depravity, including the noetic effects of sin. So then, the regenerate individual is enlightened intellectually in a way that the unregenerate is not.

To couch the discussion in the terms of "inability" and "impossibility," as above, in regeneration God does that which is impossible for man to do—heals his inability.[15] Everything that a human being is and does can be classified into one of the following categories: thought (intellect, belief), feeling (emotions, affections), or action (will). Sin affects each of

11. Warfield, "A Review of *De Zekerheid Des Geloofs*," 115–16.
12. John 3:1–15.
13. 2 Cor 5:17, ESV.
14. Berkhof, *Systematic Theology*, 469.
15. Matt 19:26; Mark 10:27; Luke 18:27.

these aspects of the human being. Regeneration redeems, or heals, everything that the human being *is* so that, in turn, what the human being *does* is changed. In regeneration God enlightens the human mind, sets the heart on right affections, and gives the will an aversion to evil and an inclination towards good. The enlightenment of the human mind in regeneration enables man to begin to rightly understand general revelation and to discern the truth about the person and work of God rightly and readily. The enlightenment of the human mind in the regenerate individual is not exhaustive. Regeneration does not immediately impart the ability to know everything and to perfectly obey God. The regenerate individual's knowledge of both general and special revelation amounts to an increased ability to rightly discern truth.[16] The regenerate individual must still learn of and grow in such knowledge. Paul Helseth, addressing the views of Archibald Alexander, explains the noetic effects of regeneration as such,

> In short, the Spirit renders sinners 'impressible' by divine truth by implanting a 'principle of holiness that restores—at least in part—'the image of God, lost by the fall.' It is this 'partial restoration of the lost image of God,' then, that not only frees 'the rational powers [of the soul] . . . from misdirection of evil motives' so that they can 'act more correctly,' it is also that which disposes regenerated sinners to 'a sincere love of the truth,' the kind of love that informs the impartial analysis of what God has revealed. According to Alexander, 'The genuine love of the truth makes its possessor willing to relinquish his most cherished opinions as soon as it shall be satisfactorily demonstrated that they are not true.[17]

Thus, regeneration does not impart, nor does it make possible, exhaustive knowledge of God and his creation, for only God is able to possess such exhaustive knowledge. Nevertheless, regeneration does effect a real change in the human mind. Thus, Paul can speak of the regenerate person as having "the mind of Christ."[18] So, the regenerate individual is able to see that all creation reveals certain truths about God precisely because God created it and is acting in the regenerated sinner, giving him or her accurate understanding. So the regenerate individual

16. "Special revelation" refers to the Holy Bible.
17. Helseth, *"Right Reason" and the Princeton Mind*, 33.
18. 1 Cor 2:16.

can proclaim, with the Psalmist, "Of old you laid the foundation of the earth, and the heavens are the work of your hands."[19] In other words, regeneration also enables the individual to rightly see the Bible for what it is: the infallible, inerrant word of God, "the only rule of faith and obedience."[20] As a result, the regenerate individual is able to see that the biblical understanding of the creation is the correct understanding. So, by the power of the Holy Spirit working through the Scriptures, the regenerate individual is able to learn *how* and *why* the creation exists within an integrated and coherent system.

While regeneration enlightens the human mind to certain truths about the creation, salvation is not based on a perfect understanding of the creation; that is, a completely accurate theology is not necessary for salvation. A right belief about, and a right faith in, the person and work of Jesus Christ is alone necessary for salvation. Thus, it is possible for an individual to be regenerate and yet not have an accurate understanding of a great many things concerning God and his creation—this fact is the basis for Christian education in general, whether it is Christian schooling, youth group, Sunday school, or Bible studies. Furthermore, this means that Christian education in all its forms requires an ongoing transformation, namely, the sanctification of both the teacher and the student, a fact that will be expounded in later chapters.

THE FRAGMENTED MIND OF THE UNREGENERATE MAN

In his book *The Universe Next Door: A Basic Worldview Catalog*, James Sire writes that a worldview—the framework by and through which an individual understands and organizes reality—is comprised of the answers to seven foundational questions about life: What is prime reality—the really real?[21] What is the nature of external reality, that is, the world around us? What is a human being? What happens to a person at death? Why is it possible to know anything at all? How do we know what is right and wrong? What is the meaning of human history?[22] The Bible has answers to each of these questions. As the Christian grows in

19. Ps 102:25, ESV.

20. Westminster Larger Catechism, question 3. This is not to say that all regenerate people *will* have this view, but rather that if they do, it is the result of regeneration.

21. Or, what is the source of reality itself; what is that without which nothing else would exist (in Latin, the *sine qua non* of reality)?

22. Sire, *The Universe Next Door*, 20.

understanding the word of God, he or she will be able to answers these questions with varying degrees of accuracy and certainty.

However, because of the noetic effects of sin, the unregenerate person is unable to rightly discern the truth of God revealed in the creation in a way that leads to saving faith in Jesus, and he or she does not accept the truthfulness and trustworthiness of Scripture. So, the unregenerate must try to form a worldview without consciously resorting to Scripture and without willingly submitting to Jesus' lordship in all things, using only that knowledge about the universe that he is able to glean on his own.[23] This means that one of the major goals of education for the unregenerate is to manufacture a coherent worldview; in short, to integrate reality into a coherent system. The presupposition that it is man's responsibility to manufacture a coherent worldview on his own, has led to the development of certain methods and models that have dominated secular education for centuries.[24] That is, the unregenerate have developed models and methods of education by relying upon their own systems of thought without intentional recourse to the Bible and the work of God's Spirit. Therefore, the models and methods of education developed by the unregenerate, and the motives for them, should not be those of the Christian. But sadly, all too often, there is very little appreciable difference between Christian and non-Christian schools with respects to models, methods, and motives. When parents who send their children to Christian schools are primarily concerned about whether they get into a college with a lofty reputation so that they may "get ahead" in the race for financial well being and public prestige, it ought to be obvious that biblical motives have been left far behind.

THE HEART OF THE MATTER

The problem is that Christian education, although born out of noble motives, adopted the non-Christian model of education and many of the non-Christian methods of education. When Christians adopt un-

---

23. The issue is what the unregenerate person is consciously and willingly doing. All accurate knowledge is faithful to Scripture, so the unregenerate person is, in part, still faithful to Scripture. The implication that follows from creation having been integrated by God and revealing him is that no one can have any accurate knowledge in it without this being ultimately rooted in God and supported by Scripture.

24. See chapter 2 for an overview of the philosophical and presuppositional developments that underscore what has been here called "secular" education. Dennison, *A Christian Approach to Interdisciplinary Studies*, 1–46.

regenerate methods of and models for education they end up adopting, also, the unregenerate presuppositions that undergird such methods and models. Not the least of these is the presupposition that it is man's job to measure, manipulate, manufacture, and manage all of reality, as reflected in the propensity toward integration as a methodology within many Christian schools today. Therefore, if Christian schooling is going to be truly Christian, it must embrace systemic change. The way that many Christian schools operate must change, as must their understanding of their role and purpose, of their strengths and limitations, and of what they can and cannot do and how to go about doing what is in their power. In short, the Christian school needs a better understanding of itself—what it is today, and what it ought to be.

5

The Teacher Is the Class

*Christianity is not merely a program of conduct;
it is the power of a new life.*[1]

—B. B. WARFIELD

WHEN I (DAVID) WAS a boy I used to watch grown men hit a golf ball, and think, "Man, you have to be really strong and swing fast to hit the ball really far." When I began to learn how to play golf several years later, I came to realize that my perception of what I was supposed to do with the club was incorrect. Hitting a golf ball is not a matter of needing great strength and exerting strenuous effort in swinging very hard or fast; it is primarily a matter of things like technique, concentration, and relaxation. Hitting a golf ball—well—is truly a full-body activity. In fact, it was when I learned how important one's hips are to hitting a golf ball, and how important it is to synchronize all aspects of one's swing, that I began to hit the ball straight and far. Unfortunately, I just cannot do it consistently (but that is another issue).

Education is a lot like hitting a golf ball. It is easy to think that it is about one thing when in fact it is really about something else. As we have already seen, all branches of human knowledge are inherently theological. The Bible teaches that God created everything and that all he created reveals him (Gen 1–2; Col 1:15–20; Rom 1:20–21; John 1:1–5; Heb 1:1–4). All creation is unified and organic, or living. God created humans as male and female in his image, with knowledge, righteousness, and holiness, and with dominion—which does not mean exploitation—over "the fish of the seas, the birds of the air, and over everything that

1. Warfield, "Christianity and Our Times," 47.

creeps on the earth" (Gen 1:26–28). As male and female, humans are to "be fruitful, multiply, fill the earth and subdue it" (Gen. 1:27). This means that there is a bounty and beauty, as Meredith Kline stated, that is to be cultivated and harnessed for the good of others and God's glory, and this requires much learning.[2] This learning is central to the biblical conception of discipleship, and therefore the biblical doctrine of salvation. Biblical discipleship clarifies for us what the "everyday things of life" have to do with our relationship to God. The biblical doctrine of redemption is only rightly understood as integral to the biblical doctrine of creation. Among the many ways this can be seen in Scripture is the use of *Yahweh Elohim* in Genesis 2 and 3. *Elohim*, the God who created, is also *Yahweh*, the one who rescued his covenant people from their captors; the redeemer is the Creator. A Christian view of education amounts to biblical discipleship, which takes into account God's roles as creator and redeemer and the implications for all of life.

SALVATION: FROM DISINTEGRATION TO REINTEGRATION

The question remains, though: In what precise way is every learning endeavor or educational pursuit theological? In other words, how exactly is God revealed as both Creator and redeemer in the learning and teaching of every subject discipline? In short, the redeemer rescues from sin so that the objects of his mercy are enabled to understand and live in creation with increasing obedience to him. This means that salvation is not just a way to have one's sins forgiven so that one can go to heaven when one dies. Salvation certainly includes the latter, but a biblical view of salvation requires us to recognize that having our sins forgiven, and being brought into fellowship with God the Father through Jesus the Son by the power of the Holy Spirit, will result in an increasing understanding of oneself and the rest of creation through this very fellowship with God. This process of increased understanding results in more faithful obedience to God in the historical circumstances of one's life. Put another way, the creator and redeemer gives the true Christian an improved understanding of the God-created integration and how that integration is related to the Christian. Growth as a Christian amounts to repenting of failure to believe the truth about the God-created integration and living in a more harmonious way with that integration. This takes place as God transforms the Christian through the Christian's participation in the

2. Kline, *Kingdom Prologue.*

Holy Spirit's merciful work. This is what Paul communicates in Romans 12:1–2. Because every subject discipline reveals God, all teachers in every subject discipline must have as their ultimate goal speaking the truth about their subject and modeling for their students what it looks like to grow in knowledge of and obedience to the integration that their subject matter reveals. By the very nature of the case this highlights the union of the integration of the subject matter with the integration existing between the people involved in the teaching and learning event. In other words, every aspect of the teaching and learning event is a living reality. Through the subject matter, God is confronting and challenging both the teacher and the student, or the parent and the child, with both their relationships to him and each other. In this way, it can be seen that every subject discipline and the learning of it is a matter of biblical discipleship or, in other words, true worship. The God who has integrated all things reintegrates us in saving us, and thereby enables us to recognize and respond in harmony with his already created integration. This results in, and is driven by, love for the Integrator and Reintegrator (God), the integration itself (creation or all subject disciplines), and those who need to be reintegrated (sinners).

THE INTEGRATED NATURE OF OUR KNOWLEDGE

To better understand these matters, it will help us to see some of the ways in which God has integrated us to the rest of his creation in our knowledge of it. The attempt to address these matters can be daunting because we are dealing with God. While very large and intricate works have been written on a biblical view of knowledge and its organic correlate, systematic theology, our desire is to confine our thoughts to how the central features of theology might bring Christian educators' views of and practices in education more in line with Scripture.[3] There are vital truths to recognize and retain in one's thinking regarding the theological nature of education. We will not exhaust the implications of these issues, because God is infinite and eternal. Still, this does not mean we cannot say true things that will move us in the right directions. We therefore

---

3. See the following works by Warfield: "The Idea of Systematic Theology," "The Task and Method of Systematic Theology," "The Indispensableness of Systematic Theology to the Preacher," "Theology A Science," "Authority, Intellect, Heart," "The Biblical Idea of Revelation," "The Idea of Revelation and the Theories of Revelation"; see also Frame, *The Doctrine of the Knowledge of God*; Frame, *The Doctrine of God*; Kelly, *Systematic Theology*; Muller, *Post-Reformation Reformed Dogmatics*.

believe, along with a number of others, that there is not only sufficient reason to persevere in attempting to discern a Christian view of all subject matters, but that this is simply about thinking and living obediently to God in his world. The idea that we should eschew the pursuit of a Christian view of any subject matter is to affirm, at the very least, that Christianity has little, if any, practical relevance in God's world that can be known—hardly a viable option for those who know Jesus as Lord of the cosmos, because he has, is, and will reveal himself.[4] It was hardly the belief of countless numbers of our brothers and sisters in Christ who came before us. By recognizing that past Christians believed in the practical relevance of Christianity to all life, we are reminded that God has been at work throughout the church's history, making himself known. If many in our own day seem to have lost their way, then perhaps it is time to look at some of our great ancestral heritage to place ourselves on right and good paths.

Many in the church today are doing just that, and one from whom we can learn much is the late nineteenth- and early twentieth-century theologian B. B. Warfield. Warfield, in particular, is helpful because he was addressing the very fragmented, neo-Kantian view of knowledge that disconnects "facts" from "values," or presumes the radical disintegration of the objective aspect of knowledge from its subjective aspect (to which we referred in chapter 2). It is this presumption of disintegration that controls much of the philosophy and practices of K–12 Christian schooling in

---

4. Hart, "Christian Scholars, Secular Universities and the Problem of the Antithesis," 383–402; Davis, "Contra Hart: Christian Scholars Should not Throw in the Towel," 187–200. Perhaps a good bit of the problem is in too often allowing non-Christians to set the agenda for Christians. If Christians, especially those in academia, would start with the clear biblical truths that God is real, that he is known (and his creation reveals him), that he has spoken through his prophets and apostles, and that Jesus did rise from the dead, they would work with questions such as: In what ways does the creation reveal God? How do the various subject matters help us understand God better? How does history demonstrate that the faithful preaching of God's word makes a society fruitful? Rather than conceding to non-Christian or unbiblical presuppositions that challenge the Bible's truthfulness, and trying to *argue for the latter*, Christian scholars need to spend a lot more time accepting the truth claims of Scripture and running with them. Truly, we must work at understanding what the Bible's truth claims are, and every Christian needs to struggle with being persuaded of the content of such claims. Still, the presence of debates does not mean that there is no correct answer, nor does it mean that all faithful Christians need to see it as their duty to convince the naysayers. Just because non-Christians, or even some Christians, are unwilling to accept truth does not mean that we throw our collective hands up and conclude that there are no answers to the integral questions of our lives.

America today. However, through numerous essays, Warfield showed that the biblical view of knowledge affirms the integrated nature of facts and values, and of objective and subjective elements, because all knowledge is organically rooted in God's person and work.

THE GOD-CREATED UNION OR INTEGRATION BETWEEN THE OBJECTS KNOWN AND THE KNOWING SUBJECT

In his essays on systematic theology, Warfield followed significantly in the vein of a number of post-Reformation European theologians and explained how systematic theology was integral to all human sciences or branches of learning.[5] In "The Idea of Systematic Theology," Warfield described what was necessary in order to even have a branch of learning. There are, he writes, "three things are presupposed: (1) the reality of its subject-matter; (2) the capacity of the human mind to apprehend, receive into itself, and rationalize this subject matter; and (3) some medium of communication by which the subject matter is brought before the mind and presented to it for apprehension."[6]

From Warfield's statement we see why theology pulsates throughout every subject discipline and the entire educational process: God created all three of these realities. Thus, God is reflected in them.[7] Perhaps it is necessary at this point to mention that when Warfield used the term *rationalize* he did not mean participating in an intellectual project that was based on the idea that humans can fully comprehend and explain everything regarding the subject matter. In other words, he was not affirming *rationalism* as an epistemic position. Warfield believed that humans can and should reason about subject matters, not that they could fully understand and explain the subject matter by simply relying upon their reasoning, even when it was submitted to God through Scripture.

God is not just the *source* of these realities; God is personally present in or with these realities so that he is truly experienced in and through

5. In order to see Warfield's thought as extending some of the insights of a number of post-Reformation theologians, see Muller, *Post-Reformation Reformed Dogmatics*. See especially Vol. 1, *Prolegomena to Theology*. See footnote 3 for some of Warfield's essays.

6. Warfield, "The Idea of Systematic Theology," 53.

7. Warfield would later make clear that human knowledge is a whole soul and moral matter in which human reason must be corrected by the Holy Spirit of God regenerating and renewing the sinner. See footnote 2, as well as. Warfield, "Introduction to Beattie's *Apologetics*," 99–103; Warfield "Review of *De Zekerheid Gesloofs*," 116–20.

them. The objective element in learning can never be disconnected from the subjective or personal element. This is one of the points we learn from Romans 1:20: "For his invisible attributes, namely, his eternal power and divine nature, have been clearly perceived, ever since the creation of the world, in the things that have been made. So they are without excuse." As Psalm 19:1–2 tells us: "The heavens declare the glory of God, and the sky above proclaims his handiwork. Day to day pours out speech, and night to night reveals knowledge." Perhaps one also sees that Paul's point in Romans 1:20–24 goes beyond simply stating *that* God *is* personally revealed in and through creation, but that all humans in actuality do perceive him to be present in and through creation, and this renders every person without excuse for suppressing the truth, or rejecting God and rebelling against him. Regardless of what people claim, they truly perceive God in and through creation.[8] Paul's statement requires us to affirm that all knowledge claims are inherently theological and humans are unavoidably theologians.

We need to recognize not only that education is pervasively theological but also that because God is truly present in and with all creation, the fullest revelation of truth is God himself in the God-Man Jesus. Jesus stated it unambiguously: "I am the way, and the truth, and the life; no one comes to the Father except through me."[9] There is a personal dimension to knowledge and education that is the central root from which all learning originates, grows, and reaches its purpose. This personal dimension has to do with the Integrator of all things—Jesus bringing his reintegration of all things. The Christian's redemption, or rescue from sin, can be stated in terms of his or her transformation or reintegration, which makes him or her to be like Jesus and thereby a productive servant in Jesus' kingdom. Genuinely Christian education is about

8. One of the things this means is that we need to be careful about how much we allow the claims others make in defiance of God's existence and truth to determine how we address particular subjects with them. There are most certainly times when we do not need to "try and prove" or "argue for God's existence." Proof invariably means criteria of knowledge. The Bible presupposes God's existence; it does not try and "prove" God's existence on the basis of criteria for knowledge that presupposes that God does not exist. God is truth and has all knowledge. To refuse to believe in God is to refuse to accept what is true. The emphasis with the evangelistic appeals made in Scripture, and here I am thinking primarily of the New Testament apostles, is the proclamation of truth, or a biblical interpretation of reality. What "proof" amounts to is the dismantling of unbelief or ignorance by the proclamation of what is true, so that the unbelief is exposed as folly.

9. John 14:6, ESV.

learning how every subject matter reveals the integration that does exist, how sin has brought a certain degree of disintegration, and how Jesus is reintegrating that which sin damaged (Col 1:15–20). Since sin is a condition that affects all aspects of creation, all subject disciplines do reveal various aspects of the disintegration brought by sin and also are a means through which we can see God's work of reintegration. Since humans are integrated to all of these matters, our salvation is organically related to them. Genuinely Christian education is about sinners being reintegrated and being like Jesus as they come to discern the glories of the resurrected and reigning Jesus through their study of the content of every subject discipline.

As Warfield wrote:

> The revelations of the Scriptures do not terminate upon the intellect. They were not given merely to enlighten the mind. They were given through the intellect to beautify the life. They terminate on the heart. Again, they do not, in affecting the heart, leave the intellect untouched. They cannot be fully understood by the intellect, acting alone. The natural man cannot receive the things of the Spirit of God. They must first convert the soul before they are fully comprehended by the intellect. Only as they are lived are they understood. Hence, the phrase, "Believe that you may understand," has its fullest validity. No man can intellectually grasp the full meaning of the revelations of authority, save as the result of an experience of their power in life.[10]

When it is understood that the Scriptures "beautify the life" and that this beautification implicates every subject matter of human knowledge that has in fact been created by God, then one will understand that Warfield's point does not simply have to do with our relationship to God conceived in a narrow, privatized way that walls spirituality off against the empirical realities of life. The God who transforms sinners to be like him is giving them, in this transformation, the ability to understand and live the truth in the totality of life.

---

10. Warfield, "Authority, Intellect, Heart," 671. This emphasis on the subjective aspect to truth and knowledge permeates Warfield's writings. For a fuller discussion of it as it relates to the Old Princeton theologians, see Helseth, "Right Reason" and the Princeton Mind. For an excellent summary of Warfield's theology, see Zaspel, The Theology of B. B. Warfield. For Warfield's view of apologetics and how it affected the scope and nature of his scholarship, see Smith, B. B. Warfield's Scientifically Constructive Theological Scholarship.

TRANSFORMER OR TRANSFORMED?

Should Christian educators, then, place a greater emphasis on the believer's transformation of the culture, or on submitting to Jesus' transformation of his people? While much of the emphasis in the contemporary evangelical community is on the church and the academy "transforming" the culture, the emphasis in Scripture is on Jesus' transformation of his disciples. Nowhere is the church commanded to "transform" or "redeem" the culture, nor is this goal the necessary implication of God's redemption of all creation.[11] To be sure, the true disciple will be salt and light, but when Jesus mentions this in Matthew 5, he is stating what the true disciple *is*; he is not commanding us to become salt and light. Instead, the point is that if we are truly his disciples, we *already are salt and light*, and we will have a particular effect that is not necessarily, or even primarily, about the church collectively or the individual Christian changing the broader culture.[12] Just as many in evangelical circles think Christians need to integrate Christian faith with learning—and fail to recognize their proper responsibility to discern an already existing integration—so, too, there is too often a failure to recognize that God has already made his children salt and light.

Our focus is not to be on *doing* in order to achieve measurable results that we call "transforming" the culture. While the contemporary American evangelical orientation seems to be in harmony with the activism of the broader culture, and therefore strives to "bring the kingdom of God," the emphasis in Scripture is that God brings his kingdom by transforming his disciples.[13] Some will argue that God is at work redeeming all things in creation *through* his church, which we are not denying. Yet, nowhere in Scripture are we taught that God's redemption assures that measurably significant changes will take place in our particular lo-

---

11. Frankly, we exhibit a rather stunning hubris when we, who do not even know what we truly need in terms of the specific details of our lives so that we may be transformed to be like Jesus, have the audacity to think that we can both figure out and implement the necessary steps for the "transformation" of any part of a culture, let alone a culture in its entirety.

12. For the broader discussion on these matters, see Carson, *Christ and Culture Revisited.*

13. This pattern of thought and the actions that stream from it are revealed in the leadership that too often prevails in many churches. The result is leaders who think it is their job to bring about certain results, to bring an agenda and enact it, even to purify the church. It is deeply and sadly humanistic, and more importantly, sinful.

cation or the broader culture as a whole.[14] The Christian's *emphasis* is not
to bring transformation to the culture but to submit to God's transformation of him or her.[15] Interestingly, the Greek term *metamorphoō*[set
macron over o] (meaning "transform") is used in Scripture only to refer
to something God does or brings.[16] The church does not bring transformation. God does, and *what it looks like* and *when it comes* is determined
by God, not by the church. Furthermore, it is God's children who are
the objects of God's transformation, not the culture.[17] Truly, the physical creation as a whole is rescued from its bondage to decay by God, as
Paul stresses in Romans 8, but again, this is something God does, and
the object mentioned is not human culture but the physical creation.
Of course, it does not follow from all of this that we are to ignore the
influences of sin within our culture, or to fail to work for righteousness
and justice whenever and wherever we can. In fact, the way we discern
who is being transformed, who is a true child of God, is by the fruit of
his or her life or actions. In part this does mean responding to the needs
around us.

14. For some clear and helpful points of application regarding this point, see Carson,
Christ & Culture Revisited, 195–203.

15. Among other ways, this emerges clearly in the fact that in both Rom 12:2 and 2
Cor 3:18, the verb for "transformed" is a present passive. Thus, in Romans, Christians
are called to actively submit themselves to a process accomplished by God upon them,
and in 2 Corinthians, Paul is simply affirming what is happening to the Christian.
Similarly, in Phil 3:20–21, Paul emphasizes that the true identity of the Christian is
located in heaven and that, in the meantime, the Christian awaits Jesus exercising his
power to transform the Christian, a power that only Jesus has and will apply in its full-
ness in the future, which is why true Christians *await* their Savior. Paul's logical application of the truth affirmed in Phil 3:20–21 is found in 4:1—stand firm in the Lord. That
this has to do with enduring the sufferings that come from not compromising either the
gospel message or living by its message is apparent from Paul's words in Phil 3:1–11. It
also has to do with patiently persevering in submitting to God through exposure to the
Scriptures for the renewal of the mind (Rom 12:2).

16. Mark 9:2; Matt 17:2; 2 Cor 3:18; Rom. 12:2.

17. For a piercing critique of contemporary attempts to engage in this cultural
transformation by "rethinking" the practices of the church present in many Christian
education circles, see Wells, *The Courage To Be Protestant*, 209–48. Wells is not specifically addressing Christian education. We identify his analysis as relevant to Christian
education. For the full force of Wells' critique of American evangelicalism, see *No Place
for Truth; God in the Wasteland; Losing Our Virtue; Above All Earthly Pow'rs*.

CLARIFYING BIBLICAL DISCIPLESHIP

People being transformed by God *do* respond to the needs around them—this is the clear message of the New Testament.[18] Biblically faithful discipleship to the Lord Jesus is about the Creator and Redeemer recreating or reintegrating dead sinners and causing them to think, feel, and act in an integrated way with God's truth.[19] Because God identifies himself as the Truth and the Word (John 14:6; 1:1–5) who transforms, it is perhaps through the character of truth, or God's Word, and our submission to it that we can most accurately understand how transformation or reintegration takes place with sinners. This should help clarify for us what Christian educators should pursue.

THE TRUTH, OR THE WORD OF GOD, TRANSFORMS

Truth has a *propositional* character to it in that it is written; is manifested in a *person*, the Lord Jesus; and is *productive*, bringing change that is revealed in what we *practice*.[20] The redeemed or reintegrated sinner is learning, loving, and living truth through the Spirit of Truth (John 16:13; 1 Cor 2:12–16), and through this is learning more of the integration present in creation and discerning how he or she is integrated with their place in God's creation (Rom 12:2).

The productive nature of truth received through God's word and delivered by God's messenger is communicated in Paul's words to the Christians in Thessalonica: "And we also thank God constantly for this, that when you received the word of God, which you heard from us, you

18. Countless examples can be cited that teach this truth either through an explicit positive endorsement of it or through an implicit stating of it through its negative counterpart. The following are representative examples: Matt 5:13–16; 7:15–20; 12:33–37; 15:13; Rom 12:1–21; 2 Cor 8:1–9; the whole book of James; 1 John 2:3; 3:16–24.

19. This can be readily seen from what are commonly called the "ethical" portions of the New Testament letters. One sees the pattern quite clearly in several of Paul's letters, but it is present as well in the writings of James, Peter, and John. Doctrinal beliefs that are true concerning God the Father, Son, and Holy Spirit lead to particular behaviors that encompass the totality of life.

20. Here we are not using *propositional* in a narrow or technical sense to refer to simply a *proposition* but in a broad sense to refer to the reality that God's truth can be written. The Bible equates God's written word with God's flesh, the Word—that is, Jesus; it never sets them against each other, as is done in the Protestant Liberal theology rooted in Kant and Schleiermacher and in many manifestations of neo-Orthodox theology that follow and are variously rooted in the work of Karl Barth. For some of the ways these have manifested themselves in Europe and America over the past two hundred years, see Dorrien, *The Making of American Liberal Theology.*

accepted it not as the word of men but as what it really is, the word of God, *which is at work* in you believers" (1 Thess 2:13, emphasis added). Of course, Paul makes reference to what they *heard* when God's word was proclaimed, but such words were not only the proclaiming of the authoritative interpretation of God's written word but also the authoritative interpretation of Jesus' fulfillment of it that his apostles then committed to writing. Thus, Paul tells Timothy (2 Tim 4:1) to preach that word because of what it is—God-breathed—and what it does—teaches, reproves, corrects, and trains in righteousness so that the man of God is equipped for every good work. "Men of God" first and foremost refers to those men God calls to preach his word in the church, but in a secondary sense, it refers to every believer in the Lord Jesus who is recreated and nurtured by that living and active word (Heb 4:12). This enables the sinner to speak truth in and about various aspects of creation because God's word through God's Spirit not only created life but also enables us to know the truth about it. God's Word corresponds to God's world. The former produced and interprets the latter, and the latter is the context in which we encounter and apply the former. Since we are both the products of and the perceivers of God's Word, we are active participants in God's world. Still, we can only be the latter in God-glorifying ways when we are nurtured and continuously transformed by God through His Word and Spirit.

The focus and goal of Christian education, then, ought not to be what our schools (home or traditional) or students can do to "impact the world," or "how they can engage the culture," whatever these rather ambiguous phrases might mean.[21] Instead, the focus in Christian education ought to be on all involved submitting themselves to God's transformation through his Word and Spirit *as they seek to learn various subject matters.* Any number of things could result from this that simply defy our abilities to anticipate, plan, measure, manage, and, especially, manufacture.

---

21. Such unspecific mantras are actually quite reflective of the anti-intellectualism of Western culture as a whole, which has an aversion to specificity in the use of language. Better to communicate with broad phrases that connote a particular feeling and allow people to imbue it with the meaning they want. The Bible does not warrant us to use language in this way. This does not mean that there is no place for symbolism or word-pictures in our use of language or that all our truth claims can be pressed to a precision that does not allow for artistic expressions of such truths that appeal more to the emotions and imagination than the intellect. Truth certainly does broaden our horizons, but it also propels us to leave behind others.

This transformation can take place through God's Word and Spirit by means of learning any subject matter because these subject matters truly terminate on and with the Lord Jesus, God's word made flesh. This is one of the crucial insights from and implications of understanding knowledge and theology as an *organism*. While it is important to affirm that God primarily uses the preaching of his word in his church to resurrect deadened sinners to spiritual life (and then regularly nourishes them through the Lord's Supper), we think too narrowly about that preaching if we sever it from all the historical circumstances of both those who do it and those who hear it. As a result, our life outside the worship event in the church has a large part to play in God's conversion of us and our growth in discipleship. In part, it signals why the family is crucial to biblical discipleship, and helps us see that we are not teaching or learning in a Christian manner if we are not holding at the center of our pedagogical exercises the repentance of everyone involved within the corporate life of God's people through the teaching and learning idiosyncratic to that community.

When repentance from sin is understood as the chief action marking the learning process, this repentance guides how we think about everything related to that learning process, including the most significant fruit from that process. Christian learning takes place when the learner becomes more like Jesus. This is seen in love for learning the integration that is already present; love for God, who is the One Who integrates, or in whom all things are integrated (Col 1:15–20); and love for others, who are part of that integration and the recipients of our love for God. What this love translates to is detailed by Paul in 1 Corinthians 13. It certainly can be and is expressed in a variety of ways, as the Scriptures reveal, but it is summarily about living for the good of others and the glory of God; sacrificing one's self for others; considering others better than yourself; and seeking to use all the abilities and resources God has given to you to love your neighbor. At the heart of this growth is learning that confronts the learner in his or her sin.

Thus, the biblical doctrine of sanctification integral to the biblical doctrine of creation[22] guides how we think about what constitutes Christian teaching and learning. Every school worthy of the name

---

22. It is hard to do better than the definition for sanctification given in the Shorter Catechism, answer 35: "Sanctification is the work of God's free grace whereby we are renewed in the whole man after the image of God, and are enabled more and more to die unto sin, and live unto righteousness." That this renewal is in the "whole man after the image of God" helps us see the connection between sanctification and creation.

Christian will be enlivened by the presence of God's Spirit sanctifying all its staff and students.[23] Among other things, this means that schools whose staff is confused or in disagreement over what Scripture teaches about the biblical doctrine of sanctification, and do not have that sanctification nurtured in them, are not going to operate in a Christian way. Failure to operate in a Christian way will certainly be the case in schools or families where it is thought that the Christian needs to engage in the work of integrating, and thus presumes to do what God has already done. When we think that we need to do that which God has already done we act both ignorantly (lacking knowledge of truth) and arrogantly (thinking more highly of ourselves than we ought). These two always go together. It reflects the integrated character of God's creation! While such ignorance and arrogance can manifest themselves in many ways, they always result in an overemphasis on what the sinner does and thinks he or she is accomplishing, along with several other manifestation of the failure to perceive and practice truth.

CHRISTIAN TEACHING EXPLAINS
AND EMBODIES THE "WHY"

When we perceive and practice truth, we reveal by our words and deeds how God has and is reintegrating us to his already existing integration. We become able to explain what is true and how it is practically relevant to life. This practical relevance is demonstrated in the teacher's ability to coherently explain the intellectual content of the subject matter taught and, specifically, how that content expresses the God-created integration. Integral to this is the teacher's explanation of how his or her life expresses this integration in fulfilling his or her primary God-ordained duties, first to the family and secondly to the church (we will have more

---

23. Obviously, this raises the operative question, To what degree can an unregenerate sinner who is not willingly submitting to Christ's lordship be a fully functioning participant in a Christian school? We very much like what a colleague of ours, Jim Favino, espouses on this matter, which revolves around reminding students what we, as a school, are truly about, and then asking students, Are you moving in the direction in which we are moving? Students need to both verbally confess and demonstrate through their behavior that they are moving in the direction in which the school is moving. If they do not confess and demonstrate that they are, they should not be attending the school. Parents must be required to understand this. There are no exceptions. Hopefully, one should be able to see that to the degree that the school is fuzzy in what it is truly about or in what direction it is moving, then to that same degree it can expect that all of its staff and students are going to be unclear about what they should be about in the name of the school.

to say about this in Chapters 8 and 9). In short, the teacher is a living demonstration of one who is being transformed as a result of being captivated by the presence of Jesus in the subject matter. The teacher is the class. The teacher enthusiastically relates the practical relevance of the subject matter because that subject matter has captivated his or her intellect, affections, and will, because he or she experiences Jesus through it. The biblically faithful teacher is one who you would often describe as simply not being able to get enough of the subject he or she teaches. What spills and gushes out of this person is the intensely personal relevance of the subject matter. It is completely at odds with Christian teaching that a teacher would be at a loss to explain why the student ought to learn the content of the class or material. The faithfully Christian teacher is just dying for some bored, insolent student to ask the proverbial question, "Why do I have to know this?" Oh boy, am I glad you asked. As a result, such a teacher is shaped, consumed, and energized by the subject material. It does not look exactly the same way in any two people, but it is about the teacher being the living embodiment of what the student should *become*. Truly, then, the class is not simply about a topic, but is about a person—the teacher, and ultimately and more specifically, the Lord Jesus and his transformation of the teacher through the subject matter.

Over the last several years of my (David's) teaching, the following occurred to me on a regular basis: I would be going to class and cutting it close to the time that the bell was going to ring. Of course, students who were also seeking to get to class before the bell rang would often take the opportunity to inform me of my tardiness by commenting, "You're going to be late for class, Dr. Smith." I routinely replied, "I can't be. I *am* the class." They thought I was just joking or exaggerating, or being brash. I was not. I was reminding myself of the sobering and humbling truth that God had called me out of my wretched, darkened condition to be a walking, breathing manifestation of Christ-like character, and that above all else, what students needed from me—whether they recognized and liked it or not, and despite the fact that I did not fully understand it or always like it myself—was the embodiment of the fruit of God's Holy Spirit. The Spirit of Truth was not only giving me an understanding of God's written word and church history, but radically reintegrating me and my life through it. Not just my thoughts, but my affections and actions over many years, had been, and were continuing to be, changed. I had changed; I was changing; I am changing. I want those whom I teach to know all these things, because in knowing them they are going to be confronted by the resurrected, reigning Lord. This is the awesome, terrifying, and gloriously astounding calling of the Christian teacher—indeed, of every Christian in one form or another.

One of the most marvelous truths about all this is that it looks different in every Christian. That to me is simply staggering, but it is also crucially significant, because it tells one something about how narrow and petty the process of evaluating teachers and the learning process itself often become in schools where this conception of learning and teaching is not embraced. Part of what this means is that every teacher and student possesses a qualified uniqueness and that every class is truly different.[24] Every learning experience has particular features to it that are unique; they resist the straitjacket of the narrow, impersonal criteria of evaluation. Teaching and learning are fundamentally living organisms, because they are about people and their growth or resistance to it. This can be easily missed in a culture that is largely seeking to stifle the knowledge of God. It is this feature that is virtually, if not fully, stifled in large educational environments, or by those who are oriented toward immediate results and objects rather than people and multiyear projects. In other words, most people gifted in administration can easily miss these realities because such people are good at organizing and managing objects. But teaching and learning are not primarily about the manipulation and managing of inanimate objects. It is not a moral flaw to have the gift of administration. Administration is needed in life. The problem comes when educational endeavors become so large, or are approached

---

24. This is not to be applied in a way that leads to thinking either that there are no standards by which we measure progress or make evaluations, nor in a way that thinks that the "unique design" of every individual has some major role to play in educational methods or instruction. The idea of crafting pedagogical practices or an entire school around the doctrine of individual human uniqueness is a fool's errand, because it fails to recognize that we are all fundamentally the same—that is, we are creatures, created in the image of God, possessing senses and a soul that allows us to learn and renders us morally accountable. It is not a grand mystery how people learn. That does not eradicate the importance of our uniqueness, but rather highlights the way Scripture identifies and treats it. The overwhelming emphasis in Scripture is not on the uniqueness of every individual, but on the collective similarity and responsibility we have within the possession of individual identity. It is the biblical doctrine of the Trinity that is the basis for and template of our thinking and conduct on these matters. We will explore this more in chapter 9 in the context of the fatherhood of God.

from a perspective that turns them into primarily administrative projects. Where there is a *proliferation* of managers and/or administrators that take over the learning and teaching, there you have virtually everything fit for stifling what is truly worthy in learning, teaching, and human flourishing. What would be truly laughable, were it not tragic in its consequences, is that educational administrators, often lacking the communication skills and other abilities inherent to good teachers, try to govern and guide highly competent teachers in teaching.[25]

Ask the better teachers and coaches, though, and they will likely tell you: no two classes or teams are alike.[26] The same is true of teachers. Frankly, much of the standard way of evaluating teaching, and by implication learning, likely taking place in most schools is the near equivalent of Rembrandt being told and expected to paint by numbers.

Still, while it is the whole life (words and deeds) that has the greatest power to influence and teach, we also need to be very clear about the limitations that our lives have. It is because salvation is a gift from the merciful sovereign God that teachers have a nurturing role to fulfill, not a determining one.

---

25. Administrators do have their role to play in the kingdom of God, but we should recognize that it is often at complete cross-purposes to what must be cultivated in a teaching and learning environment. Obviously, all aspects of life require some administration, but administration has a very narrow sphere of operation that deals with "management." But management of objects or records is not at all the equivalent of the "management" of people. The latter you actually do not do; people are not *managed*, at least not in the sense that you manage objects. People are individually different, and thus the more people you try to "manage," the more you engage in a doomed enterprise. Often, this is precisely what is seen in corporations, schools, and government agencies. The best advice I can give to school administrators is to ask your teachers what they need from you, and then supply it to the best of your abilities. It had better not be much, because teachers and coaches who know what they are doing, in the vast majority of cases, simply need administrators to get, and stay, out of their way. Analogy: I needed the bus driver for the track and cross country teams I coached to drive the bus and get us to the meet. I did not need him to tell me anything about distance running, how to train my runners, how to motivate them, or when to do anything. Just drive the bus.

26. In all my (David) years in education as a student, teacher, and coach—and that is about forty of my forty-nine years—I have observed that your best coaches are your best teachers, and vice versa. Of course, some of the best teachers do not coach, but they could. It is not surprising why this is so, and why young people consistently identify their athletic coaches and fine arts "coaches" as most influential in their lives. These coaches or teachers understand the unique human element in teaching, and they understand how this relates to the most practical/personal issues of life.

THE ORIGIN AND MATURATION
OF A CHRIST-EXALTING THEOLOGIAN

A few years ago, we were having lunch with a number of fellow teachers and administrators and discussing the issue of a Christian worldview. One of our colleagues who has been involved in Christian education for many years, asked the question that is, or at least should be in some sense, the burden of every Christian educator: "How can we pass on this thing called a Christian worldview? How can we get our students to get this thing called a Christian worldview?" Bypassing the rather controversial topic of whether or not the term *Christian worldview* is the best way to describe what Christian educators want their students to "get" or embrace, let us understand perhaps the first truth that must permeate our understanding as we involve ourselves in Christian teaching—no Christian is the ultimate cause of another person's grasping, understanding, or delighting in truth. No, that does not mean that the teacher does not have a vital role to play in the student's understanding truth. Instead, it helps clarify the teacher's role.

No teacher can make a student learn. No teacher can make a student embrace the habits necessary for learning. No teacher can make a student love the subject matter and love God. It is crucial that we not just pay lip service to these points, but that they condition our thinking about how we think and function as teachers. No, this does not mean that we functionally deny our confession on these matters, as in the trite saying "Pray as if everything depends on God, and work as if everything depends on you." That is simply another way of saying, "Be a living contradiction, and teach others to have a conflicted view of belief and actions, too." This is hardly a model to follow. Both our beliefs and actions must be conditioned by God's sovereignty.

A couple of years ago I met the grandparent of one of my students. This grandparent knew that her grandson liked me as a teacher and knew of my influence on him; he had told her so. She introduced herself to me, and after saying some kind things, she said, "I understand that you are making my son a Calvinist." I smiled and said, "Oh, no, ma'am. I don't have that power." We both laughed. While it was humorous, it was also true. *God* might have been using me in that way in his life, but that was certainly not the way God was using me in all my students' lives. After all, some of them were Calvinists before they met me! Praise God! In important ways, though, this personal influence toward a correct theology is central to all that is truly *Christian* education. While it is a gift from God that he may give through the teacher, in the end, the teacher does not decide whether it is or is not given.[27]

That is just it—you and I are not Christ-like in our being, and therefore we, by utilizing powers latent to us, do not engage in Christ-like actions. Jesus said that his kingdom is not from the world (John 18:36), and that the methods by which his kingdom comes are not the methods of the world. The methods by which Christian educators accomplish Christian teaching are not theologically neutral, nor are they under our sovereign control. They are not to find their basis, motivation, character, or goal within the thinking of non-Christian educational theorists and practitioners. They find their basis, motivation, character, and goal in and from the Lord Jesus Christ, the Resurrected, Reigning Second Person of the Trinity who is giving his redeemed people "the light of the knowledge of the glory of God in the face of Jesus Christ" (2 Cor 4:6). God gives this through his written and spoken word (John 15:1–10), which is applied to his people primarily through the preaching of God's word through the ministry of the Holy Spirit (John 16:13–15; Rom 10:14–17; 1 Cor 2:6–16; 2 Tim 3:16–17). If we would be Christian teachers, we must hear faithful biblical exposition consistently every week and respond to it with repentance that we might become more like Jesus.

This means that the teacher, the administrator, and the coach must focus not on his or her program or agenda, but on his or her repentance from sin and seeking to be ever more obedient to Jesus; to love students, colleagues, and athletes, and to serve them with what they need—not what they want, but what they *need* so that they, too, can see, hear, or experience Jesus, and also be sanctified. It means that Christian educators must ask themselves daily, in what ways have I sinned this day? To which individuals and classes do I owe an apology? Where have I failed to courageously say and do what I should have said or done? How did I try to defend or promote myself rather than admit my error, sin, or ignorance? As I take assessment of my class or administrative work and find that something is wrong, do I first question myself and in what way

---

27. Yes, we can speak of a particular theology as correct. If, in principle, we reject the notion that people can understand and practice a correct theology, then we have just rejected perhaps the most fundamental truth of biblical Christianity: God reveals himself.

I have failed? Of course, we do not stop here. We seek the answers to such questions in order to repent, ask the appropriate parties for forgiveness, and endeavor to do better by asking the Lord Jesus to change us. This is precisely the example that we want our students and all whom we serve to follow. The antithesis of this is having an agenda, a program to push, and then dressing it up in the sanctimonious garb of biblical language while ignoring, undermining, and bulldozing the people we have demonized because they do not agree with us.[28]

This obviously has profound implications for any school, class, or team, or for any other aspect of a school or educational endeavor. In the pages that follow, we hope to elucidate some of those implications. Truly we will not hit on all of the possible ones, but our hope is that you will think along with us as we explore together what it means that "the teacher is the class." What B. B. Warfield said years ago regarding what is central for gospel preachers is no less true for gospel teachers who teach subject disciplines that were created by and for Jesus (Col 1:16–17): "It is God's ordinance that the Christian personality of the speaker should be the hammer to drive the message home into other hearts. And it is easy to see therefore that the most fundamental requirement for the outfit of a preacher is that he must himself be an example of the power of grace in the saving of man; that he must himself be Christ's own man. [29]

---

28. One thinks of the words of the Apostle James (3:14–16): "But if you have bitter jealousy and selfish ambition in your hearts, do not boast and be false to the truth. This is not the wisdom that comes down from above, but is earthly, unspiritual, demonic. For where jealousy and selfish ambition exist, there will be disorder and every vile practice." The source of so much discord in local churches, denominations, and allegedly Christian schools is the self-centered ambition of their leaders. What has been sown in many allegedly Christian communities is the notion that the leaders need to "have the vision" for leadership. What this too often degenerates into is pastors, elders, and school administrators thinking that they have to develop an "agenda," then sell and get everyone "on board" with their agenda. The agenda always amounts to getting people to do particular things for the sake of accomplishing the goals conceived by those bringing the agenda. This too often is the embodiment of sin. We do not know precisely what obedience to the Lord Jesus is going to "look like" in any one person's life, let alone an entire community. These are not things one manages or administrates in the way one manages objects. Regardless of the leader's sincerity, such agendas, when forced upon a community, become the forcing of the leader's sin upon the community, and give license to all in the community to operate with their own selfish ambition. What often results are communities in which the leaders "play the martyr," and the shepherds become guilty of feeding off the flock rather than feeding it.

29. Warfield, "The Religious Element in the Preparation for the Ministry." Warfield lived before the emphasis on gender neutral language. His reference to "man" should

If we would be Christian teachers, or administrators who propose to lead teachers and students in any school, we must be transformed to be like Jesus, so that, by his Spirit's power, we can engage in those sacrifices of love required of us and display before others the way of life to which God is calling them. In the end, Christian education requires us to recognize that who you are is what you teach.[30]

---

not be read as a slight against or a disregard of females. Further, the context of his remarks was to males who were preparing for pastoral ministry in the Presbyterian Church, which at that time did not allow for the ordination of women. That was, and still is, not an affirmation of the inferiority of females in relation to males. God created gender. God determines what the various genders do and do not do. God's word is not unclear about what males and females are and what they are to do as a result.

30. This is perfectly consistent with Paul affirming that what he and the other apostles proclaimed was *not themselves, but Christ Jesus as Lord* (2 Cor 4:5) while at the same time calling others to see him as an example of God's grace and his life as worthy of imitation (Phil 3:17; 2 Thess. 3:7, 9; 1 Tim 1:16; 4:12; Titus 2:7). It is also the basis upon which James sets forth the prophets as examples of suffering and patience that Christians are to follow.

6

The Blind Leading the Blind

Idols are hard to identify after they have been part of the society for a time. It became 'normal' for the people of Jerusalem to worship Molech in the temple, and it seemed odd that people calling themselves prophets should denounce the practice. . . . The idol was supported by all the 'best' elements of society, the political, economic and religious power structure.[1]

—Herbert Schlossberg

Get lost in some places and you are in deep trouble. A few years ago I (David) got lost in North Philadelphia. Bad place to be lost. I was on my way home from Westminster Seminary when my normal route was blocked due to construction. I thought I could find an alternative route—not a good decision. It got so bad that I refused to stop my vehicle; I made rolling stops at streetlights and kept on going until I found police officers who could direct me out of the neighborhood. I knew that I was lost, and in one sense I knew why—I had taken some wrong turns. Still, I did not (and still do not) know which precise places I made wrong turns. On one hand, I did know where I was—in North Philadelphia. Yet I was hardly content with simply knowing *that*. I needed to know more—like how to get out, and on to I-95, so I could get home.

Teaching can be like this, even Christian teaching. You know just enough to get yourself lost. You know that you are engaged in teaching and that students are engaged in learning. You are immersed in a thousand details and variables; you are doing a lot of things. If you stay busy, speak with confidence, and keep learning as much as you can about what it seems you are doing, you can appear competent, even highly so.

---

1. Schlossberg, *Idols for Destruction*, 254.

78

It really helps when you are mimicking other teachers. When I was lost in North Philadelphia, it was not a good feeling because, among other reasons, I was by myself. Better to be lost with friends. Of course, better to be with friends and not lost.

As we have seen, education is theological. Theology is central to every human knowledge claim because God *is* the creator. Of course, if we are going to teach from a self-consciously Christian perspective, we need to know much more than this. We need to have a more detailed knowledge of theology and its relationship to education, just as I needed a more detailed relationship of a North Philadelphia neighborhood to I-95. I certainly did not need directions from those who were no more knowledgeable about my situation than I was. But imagine an even worse scenario: Imagine that I was given directions by those who genuinely believed they knew the way out, and yet their directions led me straight back into the same neighborhood. Or worse, they insisted that I follow their directions a second time because they were convinced that the problem was that I was not following them properly. Well, I wish I could say I could only imagine such a scenario.

At one point in his ministry, Jesus scathingly rebuked the Pharisees for elevating their traditions over Scripture and called them the blind leaders of the blind (Matt 15:12–14). Of course, this is not what they thought they were doing. They genuinely believed that the traditions of the elders were faithful to the Old Testament. You see, the most insidious sin is committed when we sincerely believe that we are serving God, that we have sight but in fact are blind. The worst things Jesus said about any group of people applied to those who claimed to be leading God's people and whose lives possessed a virtually impeccable moral character. Scared yet? I sure am. How interesting that Jesus said this of those who were immersed in the Scriptures and could identify their heritage with those Scriptures. That is some serious blindness; one might describe it as the deepest wickedness—although you purport to serve God, you are not only *not* serving God but you are also working against him and leading others down a path of destruction. Is it that bad in Christian education? We do not *think* so. We certainly *hope* not. Still, the reality of the situation Jesus presents with respects to the Pharisees, and the gravity of what is at stake in claiming to serve God, necessitates that we regularly reexamine what we do in the name of serving God. How about those of us who have been immersed in the Church, the Scriptures, and

Christian education? We all need to recognize that the problem with seeing our culture or environment is that we see *with* it.[2] Frankly, we see too many parallels and commonalities between the acceptable way of doing education in government-run schools in the United States and what passes for Christian education.

It would seem that due to deficiencies in understanding Scripture, many educators are unaware of their engaging in theology while educating. While non-Christian educators surely are *unknowing* theologians, Christian educators are called to be *knowing* theologians.[3] Christian educators must not only know that they *are* theologians but they must also know much about theology in relation to education. The failure to recognize the inherently theological nature of all learning, which may be exacerbated by an inadequate knowledge of biblically faithful theology, has led Christian schooling down confused and unhelpful paths. While on these paths, Christian educators have adopted many of the humanistic presuppositions of their non-christian counterparts; for instance, teacher-education programs at many Christian colleges and universities have too often been controlled by humanistic presuppositions dressed up in Christian clothing.[4] The result is that Christian schools promote the very ideologies and philosophies that they claim to oppose, and to make matters worse, too many of the teachers and administrators in Christian schools seem blind to the fact that this is occurring.

CAUTION! DANGEROUS THINKING AHEAD

Before we proceed in our main analysis, some clarifying points are needed. First, not all teachers are "unknowing theologians"; some educators, in both non-Christian and Christian schools, are aware of the inherently religious and moral nature of all knowledge, and no doubt some even have a high degree of biblical knowledge and understanding. Still, there exists a significant problem on this matter primarily because of the lack of depth and breadth in theological knowledge among teachers and educational administrators. Time and space do not permit us to present an exhaustive case study, but in the sections below we will

2. Schlossberg, *Idols for Destruction*, 7.

3. We will refer to the teacher as an "unknowing theologian" throughout this chapter. The phrase is left purposefully vague to accommodate multiple levels of meaning that will be expounded throughout the chapter.

4. See chapter 2 for an exposition of this thesis.

give anecdotal evidence of the problem with the hope of helping you better discern the problematic thinking that is prevalent in the arena of Christian schooling.

Second, Christian teachers and administrators are not entirely at fault for being "unknowing theologians." We must not forget that the Church has been given God's word and so has the primary responsibility to proclaim it. Biblical ignorance is a problem within the Christian school, true, but not within the Christian school alone; it belongs to the whole people of God. Indeed, perhaps it would be good for every Christian teacher and administrator to spend some time reading David Wells' series addressing the slide of American evangelicalism into the cesspool of modernity.[5]

Third, and this is in large part a reflection of many pastors failing to be faithful to the whole counsel of God, the problem is not that all of the writing or teaching on models and methods of Christian education are so seriously flawed as to be heretical. There is a decent mix of good, bad, and outright ugly teaching and writing on Christian education. Still, the overwhelming majority of the material on Christian education produced throughout (approximately) the last fifty years lacks clarity and precision, which results in a confused and convoluted understanding of the nature and purpose of Christian education in general.[6] As any teacher knows, whatever is hazy on the conceptual level is bound to be a thick fog on the practical level; a somewhat confused ideology or philosophy will lead to a very confused way of doing Christian education in the classroom itself (the ground level). The lack of clarity and precision in much of the teaching and writing on Christian education substantiates the claim that many Christian educators are "unknowing theologians."

Finally, understand that our intention is not to give needless offense. Our criticisms may offend, but an offense is not in and of itself bad; after all, the gospel of the Lord Jesus is called an offense. It is meant to offend in order to produce repentance. The Christian continuously believes the

5. Wells, *No Place for Truth*; *God in the Wasteland*; *Losing Our Virtue*; *Above All Earthly Pow'rs*; *The Courage to Be Protestant*. See also Horton, "Are Churches Secularizing America?" 42–47.

6. For examples, see: MacCullough, "How to Develop a Teaching Model for World View Integration"; Habermas, *Introduction to Christian Education and Formation*; Schindler, "The Ethos of a School Committed to Professional Development," 22–24; Mountjoy, "Heart and Mind," 27; Baumann, "The Essentials of Integration" 32–34; Braley et al., eds., *Foundations of Christian School Education*.

gospel (Rom 1:16) and that means the Christian continuously repents. The gospel is pervasively personal and therefore so is Christian education. It is likely that in the not-too-distant future we will look back at something that we wrote here and recognize our need to repent of either the content or of the way we communicated it. This is what it means to be a Christian and therefore what it means to be a Christian educator. The personal element is always present in all that we think and do, and we must hold to this truth more faithfully in our thinking about and practice of education. One of the difficulties with discussing Christian education openly is that so many in the discussion are heavily invested in it—physically, emotionally, spiritually, professionally, and financially. That is good. It is indeed that way because knowledge claims are simultaneously objective and subjective, and ultimately related to everything. So our prayer is that our Lord will give us all some fruitful measure of objectivity. Indeed, we would argue that it is precisely the theological nature of education that not only makes these matters volatile but also obligates us not to make them primarily about us, our particular school and job; they are primarily about God and his glory and kingdom.

THE NON-CHRISTIAN SCHOOL: UNKNOWINGLY "UNKNOWING THEOLOGIANS"

It may be stating the obvious, but teachers in non-Christian school systems, both public and private, operate as "unknowing theologians" precisely because there is no pretense of theology in those school systems and their operations. It is why they are normally classified as secular.[7] Indeed, such schools are rooted in the presupposition that "man is the measure of all things" and so, as we have sought to demonstrate in previous chapters, anthropology has replaced theology in these schools.[8] As a result, the focus in non-Christian education is often *not* the conscious discernment or development of an overarching paradigm that is itself the fruit of a conceptual root system that permeates the order, structure, and meaning of the content. Instead, the focus in non-Christian education is the development and implementation of new techniques

7. *Secular* means pertaining to the world (i.e., not pertaining to religion or the sacred), but as we are arguing, this is a perspective that exists in some people's thinking. In actuality, there is nothing that can accurately be classified as secular.

8. Stumpf, *Socrates to Sarte*, 32. Chapter 2 establishes how this occurred in the history of Western thought, and chapter 5 explains some of what it looks like in practice.

or methodologies; the intentional emphasis is on what humans are able to measure, manage, manipulate, and manufacture. It cannot be otherwise. This is why non-Christian education continually searches for and is enamored with the "latest and greatest," the "next big thing." As Heidi Jacobs claims, "Running schools and using curriculum on a constant replay button no longer works. *It is crucial that we become active researchers and developers of innovations and new directions.*"[9] Contrary to Ms. Jacobs' assessment, the problem is not so much that non-Christian schools are running on replay but that they are in a constant state of flux with no root system being nourished by the soil of reality and producing life; they are not operating in harmony with God's created reality. Frederick M. Hess states,

> Entrepreneurship is *not* about blindly celebrating innovation or every nifty-sounding idea. If anything, we have had too much educational innovation over the years. A decade ago, in a book titled *Spinning Wheels*, I reported that the typical urban school district had launched at least 13 major reforms in a three-year span during the 1990s—a new reform every three months! That is like trying to build on quicksand. It means that nothing has time to work, employees get worn out, and systems are left fragmented and dotted with orphaned programs.[10]

Why the constant search for and implementation of new programs, models, and methods? Because the non-Christian school is rooted in ideas that do not cultivate life; rather, they are rooted in the temporal and the fleeting: man and his abilities and accomplishments. Hess is right: Non-Christian schools and their operational systems stand on quicksand; they lack a solid foundation, or, to return to the metaphor of rootedness, they lack the nourishing soil of truth that feeds the human soul. What Hess does not understand (or at least does not acknowledge) is that only the Word of God produces anything of lasting worth and meaning; only the Word of God provides *living and active soil, seeds and water*. But in order to sow, till, and prune for education on the Word of God, educators—whether classroom teachers, administrators, or learning theorists—must be *knowing* theologians.

Furthermore, operating without an understanding of the theological nature of knowledge and learning leads to a failure to understand the

9. Jacobs, *Curriculum 21*, 8, emphasis added.
10. Hess, *Education Unbound*, 4.

teacher's role as theologian and to a great deal of pragmatism in the non-Christian school. For instance, whether educators recognize it or not, students are often viewed as something less than human, something like a high-tech machine. The teacher, rather than being viewed as a kind of theologian nurturing Christian thinking and virtuous choices, is viewed as a machine operator whose goal is to develop the right input to effect the right response (output). Such views of the teacher and student are embodied in the practices of "teaching to the test" and its cousin, "planning backwards," where teachers start planning lessons with an end in mind and then work backwards to determine the content of the lesson. Jacobs explains: "In *Understanding by Design* (2005), Wiggins and McTighe reinforce their well-respected axiom that we should determine 'what it is we want students to know and be able to do' before we start short-sighted activity writing for the classroom. They are asking us to stop, reflect, and make intelligent choices, and to engage in 'backward design' by beginning with the end in mind."[11] And again, "When I started teaching, I would ask myself while I planned, 'What am I going to do tomorrow?' The question revealed the flaw in my planning method in at least two critical ways . . . The first flaw was that I was thinking about an activity for my classes on the following day, not an objective—what I wanted my students to know or be able to do by the end of the lesson. It's far better to start the other way around and begin with the end, the objective."[12]

This is *not* to say that objectives are inherently evil or that planning lessons with set objectives in mind is unbiblical. The key is in identifying what is and is not a biblical objective and recognizing that at best one can only *nurture* the student toward the achievement of truly objectives. We would argue that there are two things that teachers simply cannot do, and these denials are anathema in any non-Christian educational pursuits. First, the teacher cannot *guarantee* the attainment of the most important objectives by his or her methodology. No teacher, Christian or not, can make a student learn. Of course, in a Christian educational endeavor, because every knowledge claim is ultimately about accepting and submitting to Jesus' lordship, the Christian teacher must recognize the central role of the Holy Spirit in the learning process. More about this will be addressed in the following chapters. Second, it is perhaps

11. Jacobs, *Curriculum 21*, 7.

12. Lemov, *Teach Like a Champion*, 57.

likely that much of the time, the teacher will not know whether the student will continue embracing the most important objectives. Both of these denials are organically rooted in the truth that Jesus is Lord over the learning *process* and the Christian teacher is to plant, water, and cultivate—not make the crop grow or even determine which crop grows. All of this is to say that biblically faithful teaching is not going to place an emphasis on objectives and methodologies that are primarily conditioned by the attempt to achieve a measurable result. An *overemphasis* on objectives is born out of philosophical presuppositions about the teacher and the learner that are opposed to biblical teaching. Notice how the goal of "backward" lesson planning is for teachers to *manufacture* objectives, then to *manipulate* the content of the lesson and to *manage* the classroom in a certain way in order to invoke (or *manufacture*) a specific student response that can be easily *measured*. In other words, an overemphasis on lesson objectives lends itself to certain worldviews better than others, namely, humanistic worldviews, which have as their focus that which humans alone are able to manufacture, manage, manipulate, and measure.

The problem of the educator as "unknowing theologian" is further compounded in the non-Christian education setting because of the inherently theological nature of all knowledge and, therefore, all learning. This means that all teaching requires both the teacher and the learner to engage in theology, whether directly or indirectly. In other words, every teacher, whether he or she knows it or not, promotes a theology in his or her teaching. What that theology may be, exactly, depends on the theological presuppositions of the teacher, but no teacher can teach without engaging in theology.

> Education is a completely religious endeavor. It is impossible to impart knowledge to students without building on religious presuppositions. Education is built on the foundation of the instructor's worldview (and the worldview of those who developed the curriculum). It is a myth that education can be nonreligious—that is, that education can go on in a vacuum that deliberately excludes the basic questions about life. It is not possible to separate religious values from education. . . If any information is transferred at all, it will assume the truth of certain presuppositions. Every subject, every truth, bears some relationship to God.

Every subject will be taught from a standpoint of submission or hostility to Him.[13]

So, even in a non-Christian school, which has no pretense of theology, both the teachers and the students engage in theology. Just because the teachers and administrators in non-Christian schools (or non-Christian parents who choose to homeschool) do not realize that they engage in theology does not mean that they are not doing just that. Thus, the premise of educators as "unknowing theologians" may be taken a step further. Not only do non-Christian teachers and administrators lack a right understanding of Scripture—not only do they fail to recognize the inherently theological nature of their task—but they also convey certain theological presuppositions to their students without realizing they are doing so. That is, they are *unknowingly* "unknowing theologians."

SPOT THE DIFFERENCE PUZZLES
AND THE CHRISTIAN SCHOOL

When I (Ron) was a child, I loved "spot the difference" puzzles—those puzzles where two pictures that are extremely similar, save some very minute differences, are placed next to each other, and the goal is to spot all the differences between them. I think that the spot the difference puzzle is a great way to point out the similarities between Christian and non-Christian schools today. If we were to put a Christian school side by side with a non-Christian school, how many differences would we really notice? And of those differences, how many would actually be substantive differences? We fear that the answer to both questions is: Not many.

It would seem that the Christian school is far more similar to the non-Christian school than many in Christian education realize. They are closer akin to siblings than cousins (or even distant cousins, as some might argue). The similarities extend from the superficial to the radical (again, from the Latin word *radix*, meaning "root," and here referring to foundations). On a superficial level, what are the differences between Christian and non-Christian classrooms in structure and organization? Sure, the Christian school classroom probably has some Bible verses hung on the wall, maybe some pictures depicting famous people or scenes from the Bible, and maybe even a Christian flag mounted somewhere. But these are superficial differences; they do not affect how the classroom is

---

13. Wilson, *Recovering the Lost Tools of Learning*, 59–60.

organized or managed. And what are the differences between the overall layout of Christian and non-Christian schools? Yes, the non-Christian school is probably larger, but are there any real substantive differences? Christian and non-Christian schools often have very similar physical layouts: the same kinds of hallways with classrooms branching off of them; the same lockers; the same basic class schedules that structure the day, along with a similar ratio of teachers to students. In the end, the physical space, the use of time, and the ratio of teachers to students nurture the same kinds of relationships between teachers and students. The point is not that the relationships between teachers and students in both situations are identical. But whatever differences there may be result not from the strategic use of space and time, nor from a concern for class sizes. Indeed, it would appear that not too many Christian administrators or boards have thought substantively about the matter at all, or if they have, it seems that they arrived at the same conclusions that non-Christians reached—not a comforting thought.

On a radical level: How different are Christian and non-Christian methods of teaching and organizing and implementing lesson plans? How easily would we be able to discern a Christian from a non-Christian lesson plan if we took certain Christian words and phrases out? Now, some may be reading this and thinking to themselves (or maybe even yelling at the page), "But those Christian words and phrases are what differentiate Christian and non-Christian teaching! To take out certain words and phrases is to de-Christianize the lesson plan, so of course they are going to be very similar!" To a certain extent, this is a valid point. Christian teaching requires talk of the Bible, of Jesus, of God, of redemption, of particular content. But the problem is more deeply rooted than this. While particular content is vital to Christian teaching, we would argue that thoroughly Christian education is not simply concerned with dispensing particular informational content. So, ultimately, this objection misses the point. The point is that Christian and non-Christian schools utilize many of the same methods and techniques; the way that Christian schools "do" school is not substantively different from non-Christian schools (despite claims to the contrary by some Christian teachers and administrators). Hence, the methods and techniques, the order and structure of Christian and non-Christian lesson plans are not different. And yet there are ways of thinking about and engaging in these things that are distinctively Christian. If the reader is unaware of how biblical truth ought to condition and shape ways of planning lessons, organizing schools and classrooms, and relating with students that differ quite substantially from the non-Christian way of doing these things, then that is a sure sign of the problem.[14]

IMITATION IS THE SINCEREST FORM OF FLATTERY

The real problem is that Christians in general have imbibed more humanistic thinking and more humanistic presuppositions than they realize.[15] Thus, much of the teaching and writing on Christian education is mixed up and confused, leading to a mixed-up-and-confused Christian school with mixed-up-and-confused faculty and staff; that is, with a faculty and staff that are "unknowing theologians." A prime example is found in Bassett and Baumann's "Teaching Methodologies," published in *Foundations of Christian School Education*.[16] The entire article is based on the ideas and methods of humanistic learning theorists and as a result focuses on that which the teacher can manage, manipulate, manufacture, and measure. References to Scripture and biblical ideas are few, and the ones that do exist are extremely superficial. What is worse, the authors periodically attempt to reconcile blatantly humanistic thinking with biblical teaching—in what seems to be an attempt to give their article a leg to stand on—and end up with a shallow, self-helpy result that falls dramatically short of what it means to be a warrior for the cross of Christ: "The personal family [a category of teaching models developed by Bruce Joyce] is based on the notion that reality resides in the mind of each individual. Because this view denies much of the Christian belief in absolute truth, this family of models is not one to pursue aggressively. However, some of the goals of this family are compatible with biblically based goals: for example, that students need to understand themselves better, take on more responsibility for their own learning, and strive to grow and become stronger people."[17]

They are right that students need to take on more responsibility for their own learning. But what does it mean for students to "understand themselves better"? While John Calvin argued (rightly) that knowledge of self and knowledge of God are distinct and yet inseparable due to the

14. Please note that we are not saying that such people *are* the problem. We are simply saying that they are evidence of the problem.

15. See chapter 2.

16. Braley et al., eds., *Foundations of Christian School Education*, 121–144.

17. Ibid.,124.

fact that man is created in the image of God, there is no indication that this is what Bassett and Baumann had in mind.[18] In any case, it is impossible to know exactly what Bassett and Baumann mean by self-understanding and precisely what it has to do with Christian living because they do not explain it. But that is not the worst part. What, exactly, do Bassett and Baumann mean by striving "to grow and become stronger people"? That statement, *as it stands*, sounds more appropriate for the set of *Dr. Phil* than it does for the church or for a Christian school. Perhaps Bassett and Baumann are referring to growing in faith in Christ—something akin to Paul in 2 Corinthians 12:8–10—but again the problem is that they do not clarify their statement. Instead these statements are flung around rather presumptuously with no clarity or precision. There is no biblical support, not even a passage reference, to indicate what the authors are thinking here and how it relates to a biblical worldview and, as a result, the Christian life. And again, *as it stands*—unclear and imprecise—the statement owes more to humanism than to biblical Christianity.

It only gets worse. Later, describing the "behavioral family" of teaching models, Bassett and Baumann write,

> Central to behavioral models is the idea that human beings are passive, waiting for the environment to act on them before responding. This principle violates the biblical view of humans as active agents responsible and accountable to God. *Despite this contradiction with the biblical view, behavioral psychology has been highly influential in American schooling (both public and Christian)* because of its historic roots and *its insistence on measurable outcomes to learning.* Some of the models in this family (e.g., mastery learning, direct instruction) seem to be preferred by more conservative educators. *While one may disagree with the philosophical foundations of behaviorism, the models it has inspired are highly effective for certain learning objectives.*[19]

This statement epitomizes the educator as the "unknowing theologian." In essence, Bassett and Baumann are saying that while behaviorist models of education are inconsistent with biblical Christianity, Christian schools use them anyway because they are measurable and because it seems to be highly effective in certain areas. But the point has already

18. See Calvin's *Institutes of the Christian Religion* I.1.i–iii.

19. Braley et al., eds., *Foundations of Christian School Education*, 127, emphasis added.

been made that models and methods of education are *not* neutral.[20] Models and methods of education carry with them certain presuppositions about the content, the teacher, and the learner, and these presuppositions cannot be escaped; they will end up shaping the learner and his or her own presuppositions in unimaginable and unknown ways. As J. Gresham Machen explains,

> A Christian boy or girl can learn mathematics, for example, from a teacher who is not a Christian; and truth is truth however learned. But while truth is truth however learned, the bearings of truth, the meaning of truth, the purpose of truth, even in the sphere of mathematics, seem entirely different to the Christian from that which they seem to the non-Christian; and that is why a truly Christian education is possible only when Christian conviction underlies not a part, but all of the curriculum of the school. True learning and true piety go hand in hand, and Christianity embraces the whole life—those are great central convictions that underlie the Christian school.[21]

It is important to note that Machen rightly states that "Christian education is possible only when Christian conviction underlies not a part, *but all of the curriculum of the school*"—this includes models and methods of education. Thus, distinctively Christian models and methods of education must be used if Christian education is to be the outcome. Using behaviorist models and methods of education will erode some of the integrity of *what* the Christian teacher is trying to accomplish, and *why*. By presenting to the student behaviorist presuppositions clothed in Christian pretense, one actually comes closer to inoculating students against Christianity than introducing them to it.

Finally, please note the references by Bassett and Baumann to "measurable outcomes" and effectiveness at achieving certain "learning objectives." This is the same humanistic pragmatism highlighted previously in the section on the non-Christian school—in fact, Bassett and Baumann cite approvingly the same Wiggins and McTighe study that Ms. Jacobs cites.[22] Thus, it seems that the Christian school is, in important ways, influenced by and indebted to non-Christian views of

20. See section titled, "The Non-Christian School: Unknowingly Unknowing Theologians" above and chapter 4 for more information.

21. Machen, "The Necessity of the Christian School," 172.

22. Bassett and Baumann, "Teaching Methodologies," 138.

education. Again, the two are not distant cousins but close siblings. The differences between the two are fewer and less substantial, because so many of the educators leading the charge by writing and teaching on the topic of Christian education are themselves heavily indebted to non-Christian educators and learning theorists, and have adopted many of the same humanistic presuppositions along the way.

GETTING THE PROPER "M.ED.ICATION"

A final example of the Christian school's imitation of the non-Christian school and of the educator operating as an "unknowing theologian" is seen in the increasing number of Christian school teachers receiving degrees in *education* rather than in their particular subject. Before we begin, please understand that we know and respect many godly, highly intelligent individuals with M.Eds and Ed.Ds. The goal of this section is not to patronize individuals but to lament the resultant shift in focus within the realm of Christian education. That is, the focus of this section is the degree, not the individual; and despite what some may *feel*, the two are not the same.

The shift from degrees in content area (e.g., math, science, and history) to degrees in education itself is not new. J. Gresham Machen lamented the shift and its results in 1933, calling it,

> one of the fundamental vices in education in America at the present time—namely, the absurd overemphasis upon methodology in the sphere of education at the expense of content. When a man fits himself in America to teach history or chemistry, it scarcely seems to occur to him, or rather it scarcely seems to occur to those who prescribe his studies for him, that he ought to study history or chemistry. Instead, he studies merely "education." The study of education seems to be regarded as absolving a teacher from obtaining any knowledge of the subject that he is undertaking to teach. And the pupils are being told, in effect, that the simple storing up in the mind of facts concerning the universe and human life is a drudgery from which they have now been emancipated; they are being told, in other words, that the great discovery has been made in modern times that it is possible to learn how to "think" with a completely empty mind. It cannot be said that the result is impressive. In fact, the untrammeled operation of the effects of the great American pedagogic discovery is

placing American schools far behind the schools of the rest of the civilized world.[23]

How prophetic Machen's words seem today, when there is no shortage of news articles, journal articles, and books published on the topic of America's intellectual decline and the decline in prominence and academic rigor of American schools. But that aside, Machen rightly highlighted that the shift away from studies in content areas to studies in education itself is indicative of the overemphasis on methodologies in education, both Christian and non-Christian. And as it has already been shown a number of times throughout this book, the overemphasis on methodologies is itself indicative of humanistic thinking, which starts with the presupposition that man is the measure of all things, and, as a result, it focuses only on that which man can manage, manipulate, manufacture, and measure. This is the core of standardization that, as Machen also rightly lamented, "is the last thing you ought to seek" while "dealing with human beings."[24] One wonders, if it was producing unimpressive results in the 1930s, what is it producing today?

IGNORANCE IS NOT BLISS

It is tempting at this juncture to call upon the many difficulties that seem to be plaguing the Christian school today—such as financial setbacks due to declining enrollment and an unstable economy—in order to put forth the charge that unless Christian schools make some serious changes, they will run headstrong into financial ruin and have to close their doors forever; that is, to make the argument that Christian schools need to make serious changes in order to improve their attractiveness and marketability.[25] But to do so would be to miss the point, if not beg all the relevant questions. Something greater than financial success or failure is on the line here, something greater than improving the profitability and marketability of the Christian school (and when did the call to repentance become marketable or profitable?!)—indeed, something greater than the Christian school movement itself is on the line: Our

23. Machen, "The Necessity of the Christian School," 166.

24. Ibid., 167.

25. Indeed, a recent edition of *Christian School Education*, the magazine of the Association of Christian Schools International, is dedicated to some of the changes that exemplar Christian schools have made in order to "survive and thrive" in the midst of an economically trying time. See *Christian School Education* 14:2 (2010/2011).

ability, as the people of God, to rightly know God and, as a result, to live in obedience to him and to teach our children to do likewise (see Deuteronomy 6:4–9). It is in God's nature to be glorified in all things; his glory is his modus operandi.[26] He is glorified by expressions of his righteous judgment and wrath when human beings sin, and he is glorified by manifestations of his grace and mercy in conquering sin in an individual's life, sanctifying him or her to himself. So God's honor and glory is not at risk. We are the ones at risk. Will God be glorified by his wrath and judgment being poured out on the people of God because they substituted humanistic presuppositions for biblical ones and failed to rightly know and live in obedience to God? Or will God be glorified by our knowing him rightly, living in obedience to him, and teaching our children to do likewise? This is what is really at stake in the Christian school.

26. Ps 79:9; Isa 43:25; 48:9–11; Ezek 36:20–23; 2 Timothy 2:13. For further explanation, see Piper, *The Future of Justification*, 62–66.

7

Sabbath: Resting in Time

*Why did the Israelites struggle to keep the Sabbath, and why was it so impor-
tant to God that he would destroy the nation when they violated it? These two
questions have the same answer. It was important to God because the Sabbath
demonstrated his sovereignty, his ownership, over Israel. Every week when the
Israelites stopped their normal routine and took a break, their actions an-
nounced that God is Lord of all life, even their time.[1]*

—MICHAEL WITTMER

THE PURPOSE OF THE final three chapters is to provide biblical guiding principles that can be utilized by teachers, administrators, and
parents to build a truly biblical philosophy of education that will allow
the Christian school to operate in a biblically faithful manner; that is,
to allow the Christian school to be truly Christian. There is no single
Christian way of "doing" school, and how these biblical principles are
implemented—and, indeed, how they ought to be implemented—will
depend on a variety of circumstances and variables that are unique to
each school due to its unique personnel, setting, demographic, and so
on. We are sure that the number of variables is large enough that we
could not possibly anticipate all of them (and even if we could, the scope
of this book would not allow them to be incorporated here). Thus, we
will provide biblical principles that ought to guide the operation of any
educational system that claims the title "Christian." How these principles
ought to be implemented will require much wisdom and discernment
rooted in much biblical knowledge and prayer. You may notice that the
final three chapters echo many of the ideas and concepts presented in

1. Wittmer, *Heaven Is a Place on Earth*, 146.

94

the first six chapters and that there is even some overlap among the final three chapters themselves. Please note that whatever overlap may exist is, in and of itself, indicative of our thesis that all knowledge exists within God's ordained system, that all truth is integrated by and in God so that there is no such thing as an isolated fact. That being said, we now begin with a brief study of the nature and purpose of the Sabbath.

THE NATURE AND PURPOSE OF THE SABBATH

The Sabbath is a thread in the fabric of creation, part of the warp and woof of the created universe.[2] Sabbath is ordained by God himself on the basis of his own action in concluding his magnificent creating work. Thus, Sabbath is a part of God's creating work and, as such, cannot be separated from the other six days of creation; it is integral to the created order. "Thus the heavens and the earth were finished, and all the host of them. And on the seventh day God finished his work that he had done, and he rested on the seventh day from all his work that he had done. So God blessed the seventh day and made it holy, because on it God rested from all his work that he had done in creation."[3]

The Sabbath is reiterated in Exodus 20, and in the process God explains that Sabbath and creation must not be separated. Sabbath's nature and purpose are rooted in God's creative work.

> *Remember the Sabbath day, to keep it holy. Six days you shall labor, and do all your work, but the seventh day is a Sabbath to the LORD your God.* On it you shall not do any work, you, or your son, or your daughter, your male servant, or your female servant, or your livestock, or the sojourner who is within your gates. *For in six days the LORD made heaven and earth, the sea, and all that is in*

2. The scope of this book does not permit us to deal with the topics of Sabbath and Lord's Day in great detail; here, you will only see a summary. For a more in-depth study, see Frame, *The Doctrine of the Christian Life*, 513–573, and Carson, *From Sabbath to Lord's Day*. Whatever one might think of the term "ordinance," the following points are clear from Genesis 1 and 2: 1) God created Man as male and female in his own image, that is, our being or person is patterned after God; and 2) What we are to *do* is patterned after what God does by virtue of our being created in his image and of the command given by God to Adam and Eve to rule the earth on God's behalf (i.e., God rules over all creation, and they are to rule based on God's rule of them). Thus, the notion of Adam and Eve observing Sabbath or resting along with God is established on these grounds. Now, what precisely that meant in the concrete details of life is another matter.

3. Gen 2:1–3, ESV.

them, and rested on the seventh day. Therefore the LORD blessed the Sabbath day and made it holy.[4]

Here, God's creative work is given as the basis for the Sabbath command to and for man. Since there is an eternal character to God's creative work, it would then seem that there is an eternal character to the Sabbath command (or at least not merely an Old Testament dispensation).[5] That is, Sabbath is a creation ordinance, and as a creation ordinance it is for all people in all times. It is not merely for the people of Israel but for all of God's people; it is not merely for the Mosaic period of history (the time in Israel's history between Exodus and Exile) but for all time. As a creation ordinance, Sabbath was required of Adam and Eve, Abraham and the patriarchs, and the nation of Israel. Furthermore, as an integral part of the creation, it is required of the Church. Because Sabbath is rooted in God's creative work, it is integral to what it means to be human; a failure to observe Sabbath is dehumanizing. Thus, it is for all people in all times.[6]

In Deuteronomy, an additional aspect of Sabbath is revealed, namely, the redemptive aspect of Sabbath.

> Observe the Sabbath day, to keep it holy, as the LORD your God commanded you. Six days you shall labor and do all your work, but the seventh day is a Sabbath to the LORD your God. On it you shall not do any work, you or your son or your daughter or your male servant or your female servant, or your ox or your donkey or any of your livestock, or the sojourner who is within your gates, that your male servant and your female servant may rest as well as you. You shall remember that *you were a slave in the land of Egypt, and the LORD your God brought you out from there with a mighty hand and an outstretched arm. Therefore the LORD your God commanded you to keep the Sabbath day.*[7]

4. Exod 20:8–11, ESV, emphasis added.

5. It may be argued that Sabbath is not necessary or that it is not required in the New Heavens and New Earth (i.e., following Christ's second coming), but even if that is true (which is not entirely certain), Sabbath is still required of all God's people from creation until the second coming.

6. See footnote above. In addition, we understand that although Sabbath is for all peoples, because it is rooted in God's creative work, non-believers cannot be expected to see the necessity of Sabbath, nor to observe it correctly.

7. Deut 5:12–15, ESV, emphasis added.

Whereas God's creative work was the basis for the Sabbath command in Exodus, God's redemptive work is the basis for the Sabbath command in Deuteronomy. The two are not contradictory. God's creative work is intimately related to his redemptive work. Redemption may be rightly described as a new creation; the Apostle Paul describes it thus in 2 Corinthians 5:17: "Therefore, if anyone is in Christ, he is a new creation. The old has passed away; behold, the new has come."[8] So Deuteronomy does not exclude Exodus; rather, the two work together to reveal different aspects of the Sabbath as instituted in Genesis 2. In the words of John Frame, "In Scripture, creation and redemption are not antagonistic. Redemption is the work of the Creator. Creation and redemption do not generate two different ethics, but rather the same one."[9] The redemptive aspect of Sabbath is further seen in Hebrews 3:16—4:13, in which Sabbath rest is shown to be a foreshadowing of the rest from all earthly toils and troubles that believers will experience in the New Heavens and New Earth, the consummation of God's redemptive plan.[10] All of this is in keeping with the reality that God *blessed* the Sabbath day and made it *holy*. The Sabbath, in other words, is about God giving power for life and distinguishing his covenant people as the possessors of it, because of how he has decided to relate to them.

So, then, Sabbath is an important day in the life of God's people, for it orders their entire lives—thinking, feeling, acting[11]—in accordance with who God is (the sovereign Creator-King) and what he has done, is doing, and will do (redeem his people).

SABBATH VS. LORD'S DAY?

While most, if not all, theologians would agree that the Sabbath was an extremely important day for Israel, many question its importance for the church. While this may sound absurd at first, please understand that these scholars are not denying the importance of a regular gathering of the church for the purpose of worship; instead, they see the regular gathering of the Church not as Sabbath but as something different, the Lord's Day. The move from meeting and worshipping on the seventh day of the

---

8. ESV.

9. Frame, *The Doctrine of the Christian Life*, 514.

10. Cf. Revelation 20–21 for more on the New Heavens and New Earth; essentially what happens in these chapters is that Heaven and Earth become one.

11. See the introduction of this triad in chapter 3.

week (Saturday), as in Judaism, to the first day of the week (Sunday) was the result of a number of factors. First, Christ was raised from the dead on the first day of the week, and so it made a great deal of sense for the church to celebrate and commemorate the resurrection of Christ and redemption's accomplishment on the first day of each week. Second, the church became increasingly Gentile, causing a certain tension within it that eventually led to the moving away from the Jewish day of worship to a day that would belong to the church exclusively.

> On this issue of the Sabbath as well as other matters related to Jewish practice, the two communities—Church and Synagogue—took up opposing positions . . . The Sabbath commandment seems to have been considered a part of the ceremonial law of Israel, as such not a sine qua non for Church unity . . . What is important for us to remember, however, is that behind the various reasons which eventually led to Sunday worship was the desire on the part of the early Church . . . to distinguish itself from Judaism and its special Sabbath laws.[12]

It has already been established, however, that the Sabbath is rooted in creation; it is part of the warp and woof of man's existence. Exodus makes it clear that God's people are to rest because God rested; that is, in resting himself God has set a pattern for his people that ought to be followed. Thus, Sabbath is integral to creation and ought to be observed by all people in all times. The shift from Sabbath observance on the seventh day of the week to the first day of the week does not change the nature and purpose of Sabbath itself. Ultimately, the day of observance is not the point. Nowhere in the Sabbath commands is there an indication that it ought to take place on a specific day, over against other days. That is, Scripture does not prescribe a specific day to start the cycle of six days of work and one of rest, only that there ought to be such a cycle. "Six days you shall labor, and do all your work, but the seventh day is a Sabbath to the LORD your God."[13]

Again, it has been established that Sabbath has a redemptive aspect, but there is no indication that the life, death, and resurrection of Christ—redemption accomplished—abrogates the Sabbath command. In fact, Hebrews 4 seems to indicate that Sabbath rest is a foreshadowing of the rest experienced in the New Heavens and New Earth, which

12. Wilson, *Our Father Abraham*, 80–81.
13. Exod 20:9, ESV. See Frame, *The Doctrine of the Christian Life*, 565–68.

is itself still future, which would indicate that the Sabbath command is still in effect for the Church. John Frame, commenting on Hebrews 4, explains,

> God began his rest after creation. He invited Adam to join him. But because of the fall and the delay of redemption, man has not yet entered that rest. So for Israel in the wilderness, Israel at the time of Psalm 95, and New Testament Christians, our final Sabbath rest is still future. God exhorts his people to enter that rest, which is a sharing of his own creation rest. "Today" (Ps. 95:7) is when we should "strive to enter that rest" (Heb. 4:11). So "there remains a Sabbath rest for the people of God" (4:9). "Sabbath rest" here is *sabbatismos*, which can be translated "Sabbath keeping," but here the term evidently refers to the future rest, of which Canaan is a type, the final reward of the believer. This final reward is to join God in the rest he entered into at creation.[14]

The indication, then, is that the Sabbath command is still required of believers today.

SABBATH, YESTERDAY AND TODAY

Just because Sabbath is integral to creation and, therefore, extends to all peoples in all times does not mean that it must be observed (remembered, kept) the same way by all peoples in all times. In Exodus 31, God explains that Sabbath is a sign of his covenant with his redeemed people and that as a result Sabbath, indeed, has particular applications that are unique to theocratic Israel. However, Sabbath, precisely because it is rooted in creation (life) and redemption (new creation/eternal life) has a *perpetual* character to it. While Paul does not mention Sabbath in Romans 8:19–23, his expression of Christ's saving work resulting in the creation's freedom from sin helps us see that all that God gave in the original creation is meant to be restored through redemption. Thus, the rest that God enjoyed on the seventh day of creation is surely to be understood as integral to what God is accomplishing in redemption. It remains for us to note some of what characterizes this integration.

The Ten Commandments outline God's moral standard, which is ultimately rooted in the person of God himself. That is, the Ten Commandments show what sin is and what sin is not (or what righteous-

14. Frame, *The Doctrine of the Christian Life*, 559.

ness is). God is righteous; indeed, God embodies everything that righteousness is; he is the standard for righteousness.[15] "What he commands of us is what he himself is and does."[16] Because God does not change, morality, which is rooted in the person of God, does not change.[17] God's moral standard is eternal; sin is sin eternally; righteousness is righteousness eternally. Thus, the Ten Commandments—the heart of God's moral standard—are eternal. Therefore, the Sabbath command is eternal.

Yet, the Ten Commandments were given to God's redeemed covenant people at a particular place and time and, therefore, inescapably had a particular application for Old Testament Israel that was consistent with Old Covenant purposes. Those purposes cannot be ripped from and considered in isolation from the New Covenant, but rather should be understood as pointing to and preparing God's people for that New Covenant and all that it entails. However, this implies that when the New Covenant realities are manifest, the precise application of the Ten Commandments in the covenant community will change. That is, the precise application of the Ten Commandments changes, in some sense, from each and every circumstance in which people seek to apply them. For example, the Sabbath, which is itself connected with God's redemptive plan (see above), will have a specific application in the period of time leading up to and anticipating the redeeming work of Christ but a different application in the period of time since the redeeming work of Christ has been accomplished. The command to observe the Sabbath and keep it holy has not changed, but how this command is kept in the covenant community has shifted in light of the work of Christ (to which the Sabbath pointed in the first place). The realization of some of the redemptive promises that are connected to the Sabbath changes *how* people observe the Sabbath, but not the fact that it ought to be observed

---

15. Gen 18:25; Lev 19:1; Deut 32:4; Ps 145:17; Matt 5:48.

16. Frame, *The Doctrine of God*, 449. See pages 448–451 for further explanation of the relationship between the Ten Commandments and God's righteousness.

17. Ps 102:26–28; Mal 3:6; Jas 1:17. Bavinck *The Doctrine of God*, 147, explains the unchangeableness (or immutability) of God as such: "If God were not immutable, he would not be God. His name is *being*, and this name is 'an unchangeable name.' Whatever changes ceases to be what it was. But real *being* pertains to him who does not change. That which really *is* remains. But that which changes 'was something and *will be* something'; 'however, we cannot say that it *is*, i.e., that it has *being*, for it is mutable.' However, God, who *is*, is not subject to change, as every change would indicate a decrease in his being."

and *why* it ought to be observed. Just as the command to worship God only (first and second commands) is retained, this does not mean that God must be worshiped in the exact same way as required by the Old Testament sacrificial system. So, too, the Sabbath, as the fourth commandment, is retained, but not exactly in the same way as required by the Old Testament sacrificial system to which it was connected in the Old Covenant era.[18]

When challenged by the Pharisees concerning Sabbath regulations (i.e., *how* to keep the Sabbath), Jesus responds by stating, "The Sabbath was made for man, not man for the Sabbath."[19] It is interesting, here, to note that Jesus says that the Sabbath is "for man," not for Israel, or his disciples, or the church, which indicates that the Sabbath is for man as a *creature*. It seems then that Sabbath will be abrogated precisely when God's people cease to be creatures. The point in what Jesus is saying is that the Sabbath was not created to be a burden to man but for man's enjoyment, for his refreshment. As God rested so that he could enjoy the fruit of his labors, so is man to rest in order to enjoy the many blessings bestowed upon him by God. However, when the *how* of Sabbath observance is overemphasized and/or placed in opposition to the *why* of the Sabbath (as the Pharisees had done), it is no longer refreshing and enjoyable to man but is a burden. Jesus continues by asking, "Is it lawful on the Sabbath to do good or to do harm, to save a life or to kill?"[20] Elsewhere, Jesus also states, "Or have you not read in the Law how on the Sabbath the priests in the temple profane the Sabbath and are guiltless . . . Which one of you who has a sheep, if it falls into a pit on the Sabbath, will not take hold if of it and lift it out?"[21]

In these passages Jesus is affirming that one's historical circumstances will, to some degree, govern how the principle of Sabbath is fulfilled. The Sabbath cannot be boiled down to rigid and narrow regulations that ignore both our constantly changing historical circumstances and the fundamental principles of Sabbath; to do so would be to burden man and negate the true meaning and purpose of the Sabbath. Indeed, if Sabbath points to God's redemptive work accomplished in and through the person and work of Christ, which liberates individuals from bondage to the law, then Sabbath *cannot* be reduced simply to regulations,

18. This is further supported by the entire argument of Hebrews 3–10.

19. Mark 2:27, ESV.

20. Mark 3:4, ESV.

21. Matt 12:5, 11, ESV.

for doing so would enslave people to the law.[22] Thus, there is room in Sabbath observance for works of necessity, works of mercy, recreation, worship, and rest.[23]

SABBATH AND HUMAN LIFE

Sabbath, although technically occurring only one day of the week, actually orders and organizes all of human life. When God established a cycle patterned after the work he himself had done, he gave all of human life a particular ebb and flow. Thus, Sabbath orders human life around the sovereign work of God; it is central to our whole relationship to God as our creator and redeemer. The cycle established by Sabbath forces man to acknowledge God's sovereignty over all things and, consequently, man's necessary submission to the sovereignty of God.

Furthermore, Sabbath requires man to acknowledge his total dependence upon God for both creation and redemption, as shown in the creation and redemption connections within the Sabbath commands in Exodus and Deuteronomy, respectively. Sabbath reminds man of his origin in God's magnificent creative work. Sabbath also reminds man of God's gracious redemptive work, which in turn reminds him of his sinfulness and, therefore, his total dependence upon God. Thus, Sabbath also confronts man with his finitude and limitations. Man's existence is not—indeed, cannot be—rooted in himself. Man is a created being and, as such, is entirely dependent upon God for his existence. Similarly, man's redemption is not and cannot be rooted in himself. Man *is* the sinner; he cannot save himself. There is no such thing as picking yourself up by the bootstraps when it comes to salvation. Just as Lazarus, as a dead man, could not bring himself back from the dead, so, too, are we dependent upon the regenerative work of God for our redemption. Redemption must come from one outside of the problem of sin, and since sin affects all of the created order (see Genesis 3), redemption must come from God. So Sabbath, by reminding man of his limitations, reminds man of his total dependence upon God, not only for existence but also for redemption and, therefore, continued existence.

22. By "bondage to the law," we mean attempting to earn salvation by keeping the law; that is, the legalistic heresy of the Pharisees.

23. For further discussion, see Frame, *The Doctrine of the Christian Life*, 540–554.

Man has three categories of relationship: with God, with other human beings (also created in the image of God), and with the creation itself (not created in the image of God). All three categories are impacted when Sabbath rest is neglected. Sabbath is the principal day of meeting and corporate worship for the Church, for hearing the word of God preached and responding aright with worship. Needless to say, when Sabbath is neglected, man's relationship with God is impacted negatively. Man needs constant reminding of his dependence upon God for all things; without this steady reminding, because of sin, man will be tempted into thinking that he is in control of his life, that he is able to manipulate, manage, measure, and manufacture reality according to his own will. That is, man thinks of and trusts in himself in ways that are sinful; man seeks to enthrone himself above God and in doing so alienates himself from God and others, because man is not meant to be his own lord. By the enthronement of self, man's relationship with other human beings is negatively impacted. As J. Knox Chamblin explains, "The effect of alienation from God and from oneself is alienation from other human beings . . . Because the self that is enslaved to Sin insists on the enthronement of ego; because every other self behaves this way (since slavery to Sin is universal); and because pride is by nature competitive, Sin's slaves set about 'biting and devouring one another' (Gal. 5:15)."[24]

So man needs the regular and continued reorientation that Sabbath provides by ordering and organizing all of human life around the sovereign Creator-King. Furthermore, when man neglects the Sabbath, his relationship with all of creation is negatively impacted. Jesus' statement in Mark 2:27 that "the Sabbath was made for man, not man for the Sabbath" indicates that Sabbath is integral to who we are, not only as God's chosen people, but as creatures created in the image of God. This means that the cycle established by the Sabbath command is a part of the created order as ordained by God; it is a part of the integrated reality that God created and is, therefore, crucial to our life within the integrated reality. Thus, in order for one to discern God's will for his life, it is important to ask, "How am I related to the already God-created and God-governed integrated reality?"

Moreover, Sabbath also reminds man of his physical limitations. Man *must* rest periodically; he cannot go on and on forever (like a certain famous bunny). The failure to physically rest has devastating con-

24. Chamblin, *Paul and the Self*, 58.

sequences. We all know how grumpy a loved one can be when he or she fails to get enough rest. Likewise, we all know the kinds of troubles that can proceed from interacting with a grumpy, sleep-deprived loved one. Furthermore, the failure to rest can shorten one's life span and even lead to death (in extreme cases of sleep deprivation). Again, the failure to rest, on a regular basis, impacts man's relationship with others and with self. John Frame summarizes nicely,

> We see how the fourth commandment, like the others, stretches out to cover all of human life. Narrowly, it teaches us to maintain a certain rhythm in our lives: six days of work and one of rest. But this is to look at all of life from a temporal perspective. Six days and one day: that includes everything. To act during the six days in a way that is inappropriate to the six days [i.e., to sin] is a violation of the fourth commandment. The same is true of our behavior on the seventh. So the Sabbath commandment mandates not only rest, but worship (the attitude that is appropriate toward God) and mercy (the attitude that is appropriate toward our fellow men). . . So the fourth commandment covers everything. Like the others, it is equivalent to the command to love God and one another. Although it focuses on our attitude toward God, it also governs our attitudes and actions toward one another.[25]

SABBATH AND EDUCATION

Precisely because Sabbath orders and organizes all of human life, it necessarily orders and organizes how teachers teach and students learn. As teachers we must be faithful to Sabbath in our classes and teach our students to do the same. This means that we must recognize the sovereignty of God in all things. We must recognize that God is over all things and that, therefore, all learning is inherently religious and moral in nature, and we should teach and model this foundational truth to our students in everything we do.[26] To be certain, we do not think that every lesson requires an explicit reference to the Bible or a biblical worldview connection, especially if it is going to be superficial or contrived (as is common in many Christian school classrooms). This is where a proper understanding of the Sabbath is helpful. Sabbath shows us that

---

25. Frame, *The Doctrine of the Christian Life*, 574.

26. See chapter 3 for an explanation of how and why all truth and therefore all learning is inherently religious and moral in nature.

all things—including truth and learning—are under submission to God. All truth, therefore, reveals God in some way, shape, or form; and all error reveals something about man and his sinful nature. The Bible gives to mankind a proper way of viewing reality and understanding all of reality; we should strive to teach and model the biblical view and understanding of all things to our students in everything we do.

Moreover, Sabbath reminds man of his limitations in time, space, and in what he can accomplish. Sabbath rest is a reminder of the necessity of rest in general. Man cannot be on the go constantly; he must rest regularly. Likewise, Sabbath reminds man that he cannot be in two places at once; he cannot be resting and, simultaneously, working. Mankind is bound by spatial limitations. Because Sabbath is grounded in God's creative and redemptive work, it reminds man that he is a dependent being and as such is limited in what he can and cannot do.

As teachers we must remember both our own limitations and the limitations of our students. We cannot work constantly; we must rest, and so must our students. We ought to organize our class material to take this into consideration. We should not give so much work that we are constantly bogged down by creating and grading assignments, tests, and quizzes. Nor should we assign so much work that students do not have adequate time to rest themselves. Weekends and breaks in the school year should be safeguarded so that faculty, staff, administration, and students alike have time to rest. Most certainly, we should strive to work diligently enough during the week that Sunday may be free from schoolwork, and we should teach our students to do the same. This is necessary for normal human functioning, of course, and it is vital to our maintaining a healthy and vibrant relationship with the living God and his people, the Church. The irony here is that when we safeguard Sabbath rest we are actually *more* productive throughout the rest of the week.

A few years ago a former student of mine (David) named Drew went to Valparaiso University. Drew was a Christian attending a school associated with a very liberal Lutheran denomination. When Drew was in my Gospels class as a tenth grader, he heard me stress the importance of the Sabbath as the fourth commandment. Drew realized early on at Valparaiso that it could become very easy for him to get caught up in the flood of activities and studies. During his four years at Valparaiso, Drew made a commitment to travel the fifteen miles or so home every week-end to attend church on Sunday with his family and to spend the day with them. He usually returned to school by Sunday evening. When he returned, he told me, he always found many of his classmates frantically studying or finishing projects needed for Monday. They simply could not believe that Drew could take an entire day off and be *more productive* than they were (he made better grades than they did) and at peace (he was not frantically busy), while they were not. Some of them started asking Drew how he was capable of doing this. Drew told them the gospel; he told them that God, not he, was Lord of his use of time. God used Drew to lead some of the guys in his dorm to saving faith in Christ, because they saw a very distinguishable difference in how he ordered his entire week. His whole week was framed by the day of rest.

The same goes for extracurricular activities. When planning and participating in extracurricular activities, we must keep in mind the amount of time that is being required of our students and ourselves. We should be careful not to put too much on our plates or allow our students to overextend themselves. Extracurricular activities also raise the issue of spatial limitations. The size (in terms of the number of teachers and students) of most Christian schools makes it more likely that teachers and students may try to involve themselves in multiple extracurricular activities at the same time. For example, I (Ron) coach baseball, and a number of my players are also involved with the high school musical, which overlaps with the baseball season by about two weeks. But this raises a significant problem: my players cannot be at both baseball practice and drama rehearsal. Something has to give; it is not ideal for anyone involved. The principle of Sabbath shows us that we cannot allow this type of thing to happen. It puts too much strain on everyone involved (I was relieved to hear that the administration was working hard on solutions to prevent this from happening next year).

Finally, Sabbath reminds us that we must be realistic about our own abilities and what we are able to accomplish under our own power. The educational landscape of the United States emphasizes what the teacher is able to manufacture, manipulate, manage, and measure.[27] But as Christians we have to remember that God is over all things, that he is Lord over all we do, and that truth and, consequently, learning are religious and moral in nature. This means that all learning of truth requires the work of the Holy Spirit. Certainly the most important aspects of the

27. See chapter 6 for an exposition and explanation of this point.

Christian school—teaching and raising up children in the Gospel—are not effective without the work of the Holy Spirit. Thus, we are utterly dependent upon God for everything we do as teachers (indeed, as human beings). This dependence upon the Lord God in and for all things must permeate how we think and act. It must shape the way we think about and understand our students, ourselves, the subject we teach, how we spend our time both in and out of school, and the nature and purpose of the Christian school itself.

In short, Sabbath ought to dictate everything we do or do not do. It should not be regarded as an appendage, an add-on to our week, or as an afterthought; far from being ignored, it should be the focus of our entire week, governing everything we do. Our whole lives ought to be shaped by the magnificent work of God in creating and redeeming humanity—both of which are integral to Sabbath. Sabbath, in all of its meaning and purpose, is what distinguishes God's people as God's people. The question is: Does that distinction mark you, your students, and your school?

8

Work: Reordering Responsibilities to the World

Instead of destroying the arts and sciences or being indifferent to them, let us cultivate them with all the enthusiasm of the veriest humanist, but at the same time consecrate them to the service of our God. Instead of stifling the pleasures afforded by the acquisition of knowledge or by the appreciation of what is beautiful, let us accept these pleasures as the gifts of a heavenly Father. Instead of obliterating the distinction between the kingdom and the world, or on the other hand withdrawing from the world into a sort of modernized intellectual monasticism, let us go forth joyfully, enthusiastically to make the world subject to God.[1]

—J. Gresham Machen

LIKE MOST TEENAGERS, I (Ron) held a series of minimum wage jobs during my high school years. In my estimation, the jobs were, for the most part, boring, tedious, and beneath me (remember, I was a teenager, everything seemed beneath me!). As I stocked shelves or unpacked boxes, I can remember thinking to myself, why does this job exist? That inevitably led to questions such as, why do *any* jobs exist? Who invented work? During my breaks, I would sit and long for the New Heavens and New Earth where (I thought) there would be no work, where I could sit around and sip glorified lemonade for all eternity. You can imagine my surprise when I learned that God instituted work for mankind prior to the fall and that as a result eternity for the believer would be marked with—you guessed it—work! But this raises questions such as, what will work be like in the New Heavens and New Earth? Why is work necessary in the New Heavens and New Earth? Which begs the question, what is the nature and purpose of work? The answers to these questions and

1. Machen, "Christianity and Culture," 402.

others like them are crucial to our understanding of the teacher's task and the learner's responsibilities. In other words, a proper understanding of the biblical basis for man's work—what man was created to do and why—is essential to properly (that is, biblically) understanding the nature and purpose of education itself. To understand the nature and purpose of work we must examine its origins in creation.

WORK AND THE FRUITFUL LIFE

Genesis 2:15 states, "The Lord God took the man and put him in the garden of Eden to *work* it and keep it."[2] So we see that work was established by God prior to sin entering the created order.[3] Thus, work is integral to what it means to be human. The fact that work is integral to humanity is seen further in the Sabbath command (see chapter 7). In order for there to be rest there must be something from which man rests, namely, work. Rest necessitates work, and vice-versa. Without rest, work becomes tedium, and without work, rest becomes meaningless. So, if rest is integral to what it means to be human, it follows then that work must also be integral to what it means to be human. Furthermore, if a lack of rest is dehumanizing, so too is a lack of work dehumanizing. Those who have found themselves unemployed against their will due to the recent economic difficulties in the U.S. can attest to the fact that loss of employment results in something far more profound than just loss of income. Unemployment is often coupled with depression, low self-esteem, and difficulties in interpersonal relationships.[4]

So, then, work is integral to humanity. But why is work integral to humanity? What is the nature and purpose of work that makes it vital to human existence? One finds the answer in Genesis 1:26–28, which explains the nature of man's work in the garden:

> Then God said, 'Let us make man in our image, after our likeness. And let them *have dominion* over the fish of the sea and over the birds of the heavens and over the livestock and over all the earth and over every creeping thing that creeps on the earth.' So God created man in his own image, in the image of God he created him; male and female he created them. And God blessed them.

2. ESV, emphasis added.

3. Please note that the curses in Gen 3:17–19 do not cause work to exist (as if the curses are the origin of work), but rather that the curses cause work to be difficult and tedious.

4. See Wittmer, *Heaven Is a Place on Earth*, 132.

> And God said to them, 'Be *fruitful* and *multiply* and *fill* the earth and *subdue* it and have *dominion* over the fish of the sea and over the birds of the heavens and over every living thing that moves on the earth.'[5]

Man's work in the garden consists of being fruitful and multiplying and filling the earth in order to subdue it and have dominion over it. It is noteworthy that man's responsibilities in the garden, as outlined in Genesis 1:28, stem from the fact that man is created in the image God, as stated in Genesis 1:26–27. This seems to indicate that just as man's being is patterned after God, so man's work (what he does) is patterned after God's work, and mankind's responsibility to care for and cultivate the creation by filling it with offspring and exercising dominion over it— often called the Cultural Mandate—is patterned after God's own actions in creating. Indeed, this makes sense in light of the fact that man's rest is patterned after God's rest on the seventh creating day, as evidenced in chapter 7. Just as God's actions on the seventh creating day have profound implications for mankind, so, too, do God's actions on the first six creating days. "In fact, work turns out to be a very godlike activity, for Genesis 2:2 declares that God himself diligently labored to fashion our world during the first six days in creation. In sum, we work because God works, and we are created in his image."[6]

But to what end? What is the purpose of man's fruitful labor in multiplying, filling, subduing, and exercising dominion? This too is answered by the fact that man's work flows out of his being created in the image of God. Being made in the image of God means that man reflects and represents God in certain ways, such as his personhood, his morality, and his knowledge, to name a few attributes.[7] That is, man is personal— he has person and exists in relationships with other persons—because God is personal and exists in relationships with the other persons of the Trinity as well as humans; man is moral because God is moral; man is able to know because God knows. So man is to represent and reflect God on earth, and thus, man's existence is not for his glory only but for God's

---

5. ESV, emphasis added.

6. Wittmer, *Heaven Is a Place on Earth*, 124.

7. The attributes of God that are manifest in man, albeit in a limited way, are commonly referred to as the Communicable Attributes. For more information, see Bavinck, *The Doctrine of God*, 113–251; Dabney, *Lectures in Systematic Theology*, 144–174; Kelly, *Systematic Theology Volume 1*, 13–222; Berkhof, *Systematic Theology*, 57–81; Frame, *The Doctrine of God*, 387–401. See also chapter 3 of this work.

glory. Hence the first question and answer in the Westminster Shorter Catechism: "What is the chief end of man? Man's chief end is to glorify God, and enjoy him forever." Man exists for God's glory and so man ought to seek God's glory in all that he does. God created man as his image-bearing servant in order to exercise a mediatorial rule over the earth for its good and God's glory; this is what it means to be fruitful. Thus, the fruitfulness mentioned in Genesis 1:28 provides a framework for all of man's endeavors, which, according to the broad categories of Genesis 1, consist of multiplying, filling, subduing, and exercising dominion. In short, man is created to be fruitful, which means living for the good of the creation—other human beings included[8]—and for the glory of God. The question now is, what does this mean for education? What does it mean to be fruitful in educating the children under our care?

FRUITFULNESS IN EDUCATION

Man's responsibility to be fruitful, to work for the good of the creation and the glory of God, has profound and far-reaching implications for education. Indeed, in order for education to be truly Christian, the biblical concept of fruitfulness must permeate it. Working for the good of the creation and God's glory will impact how the school itself is organized and how it operates; it will impact class sizes, student-teacher ratios, the physical structure of buildings and classrooms, the daily schedule, how time is utilized both in and outside of the classroom, and expectations for administrators, teachers, parents, and students. It will even dictate how teachers and students utilize and occupy their time when they are not at school.

Ultimately, the biblical concept of fruitfulness means that teaching is discipleship, a point further explained in chapter 5. This means that, for the Christian, the ultimate goal in the learning environment is to cultivate a love of learning. For if all learning is ultimately learning about God, the creator and sustainer of all things, then cultivating a love of learning will lead the student to learn about God and his creation, which will further motivate the student (and the teacher, by the way) to respond to God with loving, worshipful obedience. It is true that responding to God rightly with loving, worshipful obedience is totally dependent upon the regenerative work of God. But it is also true that God's regenerative power often works in an individual's life through pre-established, or-

8. Man's responsibility to reflect and represent God to other human beings is often referred to as the Social Mandate and is seen in man's relational nature expressed in Gen 1:26–27; 2:24–25.

dained channels of grace, such as parental nurturing, a pastor's preaching, or a teacher's mentoring. While God most certainly can—and, on occasion, does—work his regenerative power in a person without any prior preparation through such ordained channels of grace, this is rare. Thus, it should be our goal to cultivate a love of learning that God may use to call a sinner to saving faith. J. Gresham Machen explains: "It is true that the decisive thing is the regenerative power of God. That can overcome all lack of preparation, and the absence of that makes even the best preparation useless. But as a matter of fact, God usually exerts that power in connection with *certain prior conditions of the human mind*, and it should be ours to create, so far as we can, with the help of God, those favorable conditions for the reception of the gospel."[9]

By "certain prior conditions of the human mind," Machen means prior understanding, and so we see that cultivating a love of learning is vital to discipleship, for it opens the individual up to the truth about God and his creation, which may then be used by God to regenerate the individual. It is the regenerative work of God that empowers the individual to live in loving, worshipful obedience to the word of God, which serves to guide further learning toward truth and right understanding. That is, right understanding begets right understanding so that the regenerate individual is drawn deeper into the truth about God and his creation as he learns more and more. The individual is then able to further propagate this increased right understanding—that is, the truth—to others. So, we see that cultivating a love of learning takes students beyond anything that we, as parents and teachers, can do in and of ourselves. For by cultivating a love of learning, by God's grace and in his power, we may unleash others (themselves image-bearers) to further study and learn of God and his creation; this is subduing the creation; this is exercising dominion. In short, this is the fruitfulness for which we were created and as such, is liberating and life-giving. Machen explains: "Must not art and science be independent in order to flourish? We answer that it all depends upon the nature of their dependence. Subjection to any external authority or even to any human authority would be fatal to art and science. But subjection to God is entirely different. Dedication of human powers to God is found, as a matter of fact, not to destroy but to heighten them. God gave those powers."[10]

9. Machen, "Christianity and Culture," 404, emphasis added.

10. Ibid., 405.

This may seem shocking (even potentially heretical) to some, but if the cultivation of a love of learning is our primary goal, then it means that our primary goal cannot be reaching a certain point in the curriculum by a certain date, or seeing that our students achieve certain test scores, or even ensuring that our schools have certain graduation rates. The problem is that many Christian schools have adopted the models and methods of non-Christian schools, and so, regardless of what they might *advertise*, they operate with humanistic goals—such as curriculum achievements, tests scores, graduation rates, and the percentage of students attending Ivy League schools—while discipleship, if it exists at all, takes a back seat.[11] Generally speaking, the current models and structures of Christian education tend not to allow for the type of fruitfulness in education for which Christians should be striving. So, there must be a real, systemic shift in our goals and in their order of importance, which means that there must be a shift in how we operate.

Student-Teacher Ratios

For starters, if our primary goal is the cultivation of a love of learning, leading to biblically fruitful lives for our students (that is, discipleship), then the number of students in each class and, consequently, the student-teacher ratio must be low. Simply put, discipleship cannot occur in a classroom with twenty or more students; a twenty-to-one (or higher) student-teacher ratio makes discipleship too difficult, if not impossible. There is no magic student-teacher ratio that provides for optimum discipleship opportunities; to a certain extent, the optimum student-teacher ratio will depend on the teacher's skill and the students' willingness. Nevertheless, a student-teacher ratio below fifteen-to-one is necessary, and below ten-to-one is preferred. Lower student-teacher ratios provide a more intimate and personal (familial) setting that enables teachers and students to know and relate with one another better, which makes biblical discipleship in education possible. This may be the most difficult change to enact precisely because a low student-teacher ratio means more teachers, which costs more money. Indeed, you may be reading this and thinking to yourself, "That's great and all, but it's just not realistic." To a certain extent, this is a valid objection. Many Christian schools may not have the finances necessary to reach, let alone maintain, low student-teacher ratios. But this is where the *systemic* change that

11. Please see chapter 6 for further exposition of this thesis.

we have been talking about comes into consideration. Achieving and maintaining a low student-teacher ratio may require a complete change in how the school operates financially. It may mean spending more time in raising money for teacher salaries; it may require schools to rent a building rather than buy one; it may mean having fewer administrators; it may mean not having the money to buy the latest and greatest technology; it may delay the opening of a new school; it may dictate that two schools merge and pool their resources; it may mean an approach much more in line with what takes place in home-school or co-op situations. As with all of the changes that will be highlighted in this section, there is no magic-bullet solution to achieving and maintaining lower student-teacher ratios; each school will have to discern the best course of action for itself. But remember, the teacher is the class, and so the better the teacher can relate to the students, and vice-versa, the better the result.[12]

Physical Layout

In addition to low student-teacher ratios, cultivating a love of learning that leads to fruitfulness will also impact the school's physical layout and organization. To a certain extent, this also includes how individual classrooms are organized and structured, but ultimately the teacher is more important than the physical layout of the classroom. Again, the teacher is the class (see chapter 5), so although the physical layout and organization of the classroom itself can have an impact on how students and teachers interact with and relate to one another, it is not as significant as who the teacher is and what he or she does. Thus, the focus here is the layout of the school at large. A given school's building or buildings should be organized in such a way so as to maximize interactions between students and teachers; not only does this afford more time for discipleship but it also helps minimize troublemaking (because teachers are with and around students more often). One of the problems with many campus-style layouts is that often they are too spread out. As a result, the interpersonal interactions that occur between classes are often minimized. In a campus-style layout, teachers often teach in multiple classrooms and have offices that are separate from their classrooms. This means that teachers are busy trying to get from classroom to classroom during breaks, and have little time for conversing with—let alone keeping an eye on—students who are on the way to their next

12. Please see chapter 5 for an explanation of "the teacher is the class."

class. Furthermore, in schools with a campus layout, teachers are more likely to spend their free periods tucked away in an office or classroom separated from the students in some way, making them more difficult to access. Single-building schools, on the other hand, tend to be a bit more chaotic and cramped; teachers may share classrooms, so that one teacher works at a computer in the back while another teacher lectures at the front, which excludes certain student-teacher interactions. It is unlikely that a student will come search me out during a free period if he knows that he has to interrupt another class to see me; even if the student did interrupt the class to find me, we would have to talk somewhere else. So, to be sure, single-building schools have problems of their own. But student "pop-ins" are more likely in single-building schools precisely because the teacher is not tucked away in an office and so separate from the classrooms and hallways during free periods. So, single-building schools have their benefits as well. But whatever the case may be, every effort must be made to maximize teacher accessibility and increase the frequency of student-teacher interactions throughout the course of the school day.

Schedules

One way of increasing teacher accessibility and student-teacher inter-actions—and, by doing so, aiding discipleship—is through the daily school schedule. More time between classes (within reason; too much time can be detrimental) may give teachers and students the time they need to relax a little between classes so that they can converse with one another, opening up opportunities for discipleship. Another option is to schedule a block of "free time" into each day (or every couple of days) during which teachers and students can meet formally or informally. Indeed, Delaware County Christian School, where I (Ron) teach, has a twenty-minute block of time between second and third periods that is used for just such a purpose. Of course, simply scheduling the time is not the solution. Teachers have to be purposeful in how they use the time afforded them. For example, when the twenty-minute block of time between second and third periods was first implemented, David told me that he was making the resolution that he would not spend the twenty minutes in his office but that he would spend it in the cafeteria where many students who did not have meetings to attend congregated to have a snack and hang out between classes. By doing so, David was increasing the amount of time he had for discipleship. Likewise, you might have to make a resolution that you will do your best to spend the time between classes in the hallways with students, making yourself accessible and allowing for the possibility of more student-teacher interactions.

Curriculum Taught

Furthermore, nurturing a love of learning that benefits the creation and glorifies God also shapes the curriculum in the Christian school. For starters, showing the God-ordained integrated nature of all reality is a must in a truly Christian school. This means that teachers must strive to show how God has integrated all things in, by, and through himself, and how all learning terminates on and with the Lord Jesus Christ, God's word made flesh. This also means that Christian schools cannot shy away from certain topics because they are controversial and/or difficult. For when we understand that all truth is God's and that as such all truth begins and ends with him, we will be emboldened to address both Christian and non-Christian viewpoints, knowing that the truth will prevail. Of course, wisdom will be required regarding what topics and arguments to bring up with any group of students. Ages, genders, learning abilities, and life histories need to be factored in to what is and is not addressed. Still, one must keep in mind that in order to answer the questions and arguments of various non-Christian positions, we must know those questions and arguments. Machen summarizes these points nicely.

> It is true, one of the grounds for our belief is an inward experience that we cannot share—the great experience begun by conviction of sin and conversion and continued by communion with God—an experience which other men do not possess, and upon which, therefore, we cannot directly base an argument. But if our position is correct, we ought at least to be able to show the other man that his reasons may be inconclusive. And that involves *careful study of both sides of the question.* Furthermore, the field of Christianity is the world. The Christian cannot be satisfied so long as any human activity is either opposed to Christianity or out of all connection with Christianity. Christianity must not pervade merely all nations, but also all human thought. *The Christian, therefore, cannot be indifferent to any branch of any earnest human endeavor. It must all be brought into some relation to the gospel.* It must be studied either in order to be demonstrated to be false, or else in order to be made useful in advancing the kingdom of God.[13]

13. Machen, "Christianity and Culture," 403, emphasis added.

Students over Curriculum

Working for the good of the creation—human beings included—and the glory of God in teaching also means that, to a certain extent, the students take precedence over the curriculum. Again, the primary goal in Christian education is cultivating a love of learning that leads to fruitful lives, not reaching a certain point in the curriculum by a certain date. This means that there are times when teachers have to put the curriculum aside in order to answer student questions and/or address student concerns—issues with which they are wrestling. A colleague of mine recently relayed to me that discussion in a couple of his classes led to students venting that one of the most frustrating statements they hear from teachers is, "That's a great question, but I don't have time to get into it right now because we have to get through these notes." In other words, students get frustrated when teachers do not take the time to address questions and concerns that they currently have about topics and issues that are raised in class; that is, when teachers regularly express a greater concern for the curriculum than for students. To a certain extent, this frustration has to be taken with a grain of salt. Many students want nothing more than to do what they want to do when they want to do it; in the classroom, that may translate to sidetracking the teacher in order to get him or her off the curriculum because the student considers it to be boring or impractical; sometimes, students sidetrack the teacher and monopolize his or her time out of spite. But at the same time it reveals something fundamental to human nature: learning involves discipleship, which means that relationships are crucial for learning. If students perceive that a teacher does not care about them, if teachers do not have good rapport with their students, then learning does not occur. We must not allow students to monopolize class time and in so doing hinder other students from learning. Of course, when the student-teacher ratio drops to something much closer to ten to one than twenty or twenty-five to one, these dynamics change significantly. Moreover, we must realize that our primary concern is not to be friends with students; we are an authority over them. But at the same time, we must recognize the nature of that authority (see chapter 9), and that requires us to expend great effort to establish good rapport with our students, to care for their well-being, their livelihood, and their relationship with the living God, and to show them, in word and deed, that we care for them in these ways. It is through these relationships that meaningful and fruitful (in the biblical sense of the word) learning takes place.

Teacher's Familial Responsibilities

Fruitfulness in education also requires the teacher to maintain certain boundaries between school and home in order to maintain healthy relationships at home. This is true of any job, but teachers more than others tend to bring a lot of work home with them; indeed, it is generally accepted that bringing schoolwork home is necessary and good for teachers to do. On occasion it may be necessary, and different circumstances necessitate different solutions. But on the whole, teachers should make every effort to leave schoolwork at school in order to give their families their full attention and focus when at home.[14] By doing so, the teacher maintains the right, God-ordained relationship with spouse and children, which is his or her primary stewardship. That is, by maintaining the proper God-ordained relationship with spouse and children, the teacher is demonstrating the reality of the integration present in creation. This is another way in which the teacher bears testimony to what is true, to who God is and what he has done, and lives as we were meant to live. This has profound implications for both home and school. By giving our families our full energies when we are at home, we are able to take our minds off of school, granting us rest and establishing a daily cycle of work and rest that will make us more productive and efficient when we are at work (a Sabbath principle that is explained more fully in chapter 7). Moreover, faithfulness in our primary stewardship at home means that our families will be nourished with life that in turn energizes us to engage in fruitful work. Furthermore, by maintaining proper boundaries between work and school and, therefore, right relationships at home, we model for our students how biblically based Christian families look and operate. In other words, we are shepherding them in how to relate to their parents as God-honoring children, and in how to be a Christian husband or wife, father or mother one day so that they might teach their children likewise. By modeling biblically faithful Christian family for our students, we are teaching them how to properly execute dominion over the creation, as they have been created in the image of God. In short, we are teaching them how to be *fruitful*. Chapter 9 will go into greater detail on the relational nature of education and the impact the family has on a truly Christian education.

---

14. My (David's) rule was that unless it was an emergency situation I never did schoolwork at home. I discovered I had a lot more energy both for home and work when I maintained this boundary.

CONCLUSION

Education is discipleship and, therefore, Christian education has as its goal the cultivation and nurturing of a love of learning, recognizing that all truth starts and stops with and in God. For all truth is God's truth. Insofar as an individual knows, understands, and loves the truth, that individual knows, understands, and loves God. Mankind was created in the image of God and given the responsibility to subdue the earth by exercising dominion as God's representatives, on his behalf (this is part and parcel of image-bearing), and by multiplying and filling the earth. In other words, mankind is to *expand in numbers, explore the earth, explain God's truth,* and *enjoy God's bounty*; this is what it means, in Genesis 1:28, to be *fruitful*. We expand in numbers so that there are ever more image-bearers sent into the world to explore the earth, explain God's truth, and enjoy God's bounty. But this necessitates that we cultivate a love of learning that begins and ends with and in God in the expanding population—the subsequent generations—the exploration of creation, the explaining of God's truth, and the enjoyment of God through it all. This is the goal of Christian education. The quote from Machen that begins this chapter points out that only we Christians, because of the Holy Spirit's work in revealing the truth to us through the word of God, can truly explain the world around us and, in doing so, enjoy God and his creation. As a result, the Christian school ought not to shrink away from certain topics and studies; neither should the Christian school operate with the same assumptions, categories, and presuppositions as non-Christian schools. Instead, Christian schools should strive to show how all truth starts and stops with and in God in order to make known his glory and sovereignty to all peoples. Likewise, Christian schools should strive to show how all untruths—in whatever guise they may take—oppose God and seek to dethrone him (in some way, shape, or form). In this way, the Christian school will send ever more image-bearers to explore the creation, explain God's truth, and enjoy God's bounty. In this way, the Christian school is fruitful.

9

Family: A Teaching Affair

Religious communities have always been particularly unwilling to repent.
Sweeping change is more likely to occur in the secular realm; castles turn into
ruins, and dynasties disappear. In churches, on the other hand, God's name
is tied to the things people say and do, so everything they inherited from their
forefathers—even when it is afflicted with error and sin—continues unabated.
They use the truth given them to bolster their communal pride, which inocu-
lates them even against their ailments. [1]

—ADOLF SCHLATTER

T HE BIBLE HAS MANY specific things to say about fathers and mothers
teaching their children; it says nothing specifically about schools,
Christian or otherwise, as the mechanism for such teaching. That does
not mean that schools are automatically evil or a bad idea, but neither
are they mandated. Whether any school is or is not a good idea must
be evaluated based on whether its goals and operation correspond to
Scripture's commands and implications.[2] The reality of creation's integrated character means that Christian discipleship is about learning and
maturing in understanding how all subjects reveal God, and increasing
in obedience to God. Interests and abilities given by God will shape every
Christian's discipleship to Jesus, so we dare not think of these matters in a
simplistic, monolithic way. Though God has created every person in his

1. Schlatter, *Do We Know Jesus?*, 54.

2. Our purpose is not to tell parents whether they should homeschool or send their
children to a Christian school, a private non-Christian school, or a government-run
school. Every parent must make that decision based on numerous variables and a con-
science informed by God's Word. Our hope is that in some way what we have written
will help parents in making this decision.

image, no two people are exactly the same, and this qualified uniqueness ought to play a large role in our thinking about and implementation of any Christian education. Among other things, this highlights the central role of the biological family in Christian education or discipleship.[3]

The central relational reality that governs human life is the biological family, and it is organically united to God's covenant-redeemed community. We need to do more than speak platitudes about a "three-legged stool" (the home, the church, the school), or how we are "in partnership with parents" when articulating a biblical approach to discipleship or education. We only understand what constitutes a Christian view of learning or education when we understand the centrality of the biological family and what marks its union to God's covenant-redeemed community. Among other things, this highlights the union between creation and redemption, as well as the relational reality of covenant. The biological family was created by God prior to sin, and it is through the first biological family that God began to redeem humans and the rest of creation. By paying attention to what God's Word says about the relationship between husbands and wives fulfilling their duties as fathers and mothers, we are better equipped to understand Christian teaching and learning.

SCHOOLS ARE NOT NECESSARY

Dare I say it? Christian schools are not necessary for God's kingdom to come. Christian learning is. If the proliferation of homeschooling is not teaching this to traditional school advocates, then perhaps the latter are demonstrating that they really cannot think outside the box

---

3. We are very grateful for the tireless work of Dr. James Dobson and those who have assisted in his Focus on the Family. Our emphases are theological and not primarily psychological, though, and it is a theological understanding that Christians need if they are to fully understand the character and function of the biological family in God's creation. Like the formal discipline of education, the formal discipline of psychology has the beginning of its rise in the late nineteenth century. Both have profoundly antibiblical roots. Whatever insights might be gleaned from either discipline is dependent upon those disciplines being evaluated by a biblically faithful theology. As the latter has been increasingly marginalized in the West, the formal disciplines of education and psychology have gained ascendancy. These developments have affected local churches and the creation of parachurch ministries, such as Focus on the Family, and Christian schools. That these realities are enmeshed in and both influenced by and an influencer of the political and economic situation in the West seems obvious to us. Addressing the latter issues, however, is well beyond the scope of our work here.

and have succeeded in making themselves, like Uncle Andrew in *The Magician's Nephew*, "stupider" than they really are.[4] Throughout the history of the church, many Christians have understood the importance of learning, and not just learning about the Bible or the gospel message narrowly conceived, but learning about all subject disciplines, because it was understood that the God who redeems is the God who created. For centuries, the majority of educational institutions were either begun by, or had deep ties to, the church or a group within it. Christians need to understand, though, that Christianity does not just require us to be occupied with *what* we learn, but to recognize how relationships within the family condition *how* we learn. Of course, the latter is part of *what* we *should* learn! The structures or operations that Christians use to fulfill the teaching mandate within God's kingdom should not be driven by non-Christian ideologies, but rather by who God is. This follows because God is revealed in creation. Humans are intimately and organically united to creation and the biological family is central to this union. God gave the creation mandate to the first male and female, who were the first husband and wife. Thus, the relational paradigm for thinking about human learning or education is the biological family, which is a reflection of God as Trinity: Father, Son, and Holy Spirit. If we would teach in a Christian way, we must pay attention to what Scripture says about what it means to be a God-fearing parent.[5] This will move us significantly away from the way government-funded and government-operated schools in the U.S. and many other places engage in their task.

METHODOLOGIES DRIVEN BY OR TRYING TO ACCOMPLISH INTEGRATION?

Though we earlier criticized the preoccupation with methodologies, that criticism was aimed at an emphasis on humanistic methodologies that ignore important aspects of teaching and learning, while attempting to accomplish an already existing integration between faith and learning.

---

4. In C. S. Lewis, *The Magician's Nephew*, 149–52, Uncle Andrew only hears roaring when Aslan sings because Uncle Andrew does not *like* what Aslan's voice makes him think and feel. This is *because of the kind of person he is*. So he willfully distorts Aslan's voice. It is an accurate illustration of sin.

5. The person who never marries, the divorced person, and the person without biological children can still demonstrate these attributes because the origin of the attributes is God, not the human experience of being married and having children.

That faith and learning have always been integrated is revealed in humans as finite creatures who must exercise faith in their interpretation of all the data of sense experience.[6] God already created us to be such creatures. He gave us senses, by which we access physical creation, and minds, by which we reason about the data we take in through our senses. Because we are finite creatures, all humans have to exercise epistemic faith as we proceed in our interpretation of sensory data. One can perhaps see why a formal emphasis on education as a separate subject discipline is a relatively recent phenomenon in Western intellectual history.[7] It is not surprising how humans learn, at least when you pay attention to humans and do not have your interpretive judgments clouded by an ideology that suppresses the truth about God, humans, and, by implication, the rest of creation.

Those who are consistently, if not constantly, occupied with methodology in teaching are those who do not understand humans very well, and are operating with a fairly significant ignorance regarding Scripture and the creation. We submit that the reason that non-Christian educational theories and practices are enamored with methodology that focuses on how to teach people and how people learn is that such theories are suppressing the truth about God, which is made known to all through the creation.[8] Non-Christian views of reality eventually have no recourse but to relativize truth and make it simply about private perceptions. This results in learning approaches that correspond to such relativism. A Christian view of learning revolves around what *is*, and this has to include recognizing the subjective, personal dimension to learning. Non-Christian views ultimately revolve around what the individual *likes* or *wants things to be*.[9] Both perspectives—Christian and non-Christian—will address the objective and subjective elements in knowledge (epistemology); they cannot avoid them. The seminal difference is in how they understand the relationship between the two. Their methodologies will reveal what they actually believe regarding the rela-

6. The perspective on the relationship between faith and reason that considers human reason as capable of taking one to a particular epistemic point and then needing faith to "kick in" or enter into the picture, so to speak, is unbiblical. It can also be shown to be out of accord with the way humans operate as creatures.

7. Machen, "The Necessity of the Christian School," 166.

8. Ps 19; Rom 1:18–32.

9. Lewis, *The Abolition of Man*, helps reveal the descent into propaganda and the incoherency of what has been fomenting in the West for many decades.

tionship between the objective and subjective aspects of knowledge. This includes every person's responsibility before God to work at learning and to submit to the authority structure integral to the creation. Since God places a prominence on the biological family for the fulfilling of his creation mandate, or the advancement of his kingdom, non-Christians have a vested interest in subverting the authority and function of the biological family.[10]

GOD REVEALS HIMSELF AS FAMILY AND IN FAMILY

God is *Father, Son* and *Holy Spirit,* the eternal and infinite Trinity. It is God from whom every family in heaven and earth is named, or derives its name (Eph 3:15). What Paul affirms in Ephesians is that the character and function of every family is rooted in who God is as Father, Son, and Holy Spirit and in the work they perform in saving sinners. Among other ways, we see that redemption and creation are united in that Jesus is regarded as the Last or Second Adam, and the relationship that Jesus has to the Church is analogous to the relationship that a husband has to his wife (1Cor 15; Rom 5:12–21; Eph 5:21–33). In other words, in the creation, in the forming of the first husband and wife (Genesis 1 and 2), we have already a mirror image, so to speak, of the relationship that holds between Jesus and the Church. The wife is called the helper—in Hebrew, *ezer* (*azar*)—of her husband. God calls himself the same thing in relation to his redeemed people and is recognized as such by them.[11] The husband is required to relate to his wife in the same way that God

---

10. Understanding that the creation mandate is the advancement of God's kingdom does not necessarily require one to conclude that all work performed by Christians in God's creation ought to be seen as "gospel ministry" in a clear or obvious way. There are realities integral to God's kingdom that correspond to realities in Man's kingdom. The latter is certainly working at cross-purposes with God in its *stated intentions,* but in order to live in God's creation you cannot help affirming some of his truth and operating according to it, to some degree. Besides undermining some applications of presuppositionalist apologetics that want to drive a hard separation between Christian and non-Christian systems of thought (as has been done by some in the Dutch Reformed tradition), it helps us see that part of God's causing all things to work together for the good of his saved people is the work that non-Christians do. Among other things, it also means that Christians can do all their work for the glory of God and the good of others without thinking that there has to be a significant difference between Christians and non-Christians in every line of work.

11. Deut 33:7, 26, 29; Ps 33:20; 35:2; 38:22; 40:13, 17; 44:26; 46:1, 5; 115:9–11; 121:1–2; Isa 41:13–14.

calls his redeemed people to relate to him, namely, to cling, cleave, or hold fast (*davaq*) to him.[12] Thus, while the husband and wife have different requirements to meet in the precise way they function in relation to each other, both are presented in Scripture as fulfilling God-like roles.[13]

In Genesis 18:19, God declares that he has chosen Abraham so that Abraham might "command his children and his household after him to keep the way of the LORD by doing righteousness and justice, so that the LORD might bring upon Abraham the things he has promised him." Here, we have an example of the integrated character of creation and redemption, because Abraham's "family" is both his biological offspring and his servants, and they are all regarded as God's supernatural work. Even still, it is God's supernatural work that is regarded as the ultimate determiner, because biological reproduction alone was not the ultimate determiner regarding who was or was not in Abraham's "family."

Isaac was the son of the covenant promise and the result of biological reproduction. Still, Abraham had servants, and his extended family took on servants throughout subsequent generations. Furthermore, just as God chose Isaac and not Ishmael, God chose Jacob and not Esau. God's choice did not nullify the choices made by those whom he chose; it enlivened and equipped them. Man's will is dependent on God's, all the time, not the reverse.[14] Even the servants were part of his household.

---

12. Gen 2:24; Deut 10:20; 13:4, 17; Josh 22:5; 23:8.

13. Eph 5:23 tells us that "the husband is the head of the wife even as Christ is the head of the church, his body, and is himself its Savior." In other words, the husband is required to give himself up for his wife, cherishing and nourishing her, in order that he might nurture God's redemptive work in her (Eph 5:25–29). She is required to submit to her husband (Eph 5:24), just as Jesus submitted himself to the Father. For further references to God acting in a motherly fashion, see Isa 49:15; 66:10–13.

14. Arminianism is deistic, and in this sense Platonic, and therefore right in step with the "worldly" way of thinking of most Americans. Is it any wonder that much of American evangelicalism, which has been significantly influenced by Arminianism, has for decades borrowed from and reflected what is popular in American culture as a whole? The Fact/Value split popular in Western culture and addressed in chapter 2 is reflected in Arminianism. Both fail to affirm that God is present and operative in every aspect of the creation. In Arminianism, it is man's will that somehow remains outside of God's presence and operation. Once the wholeness of humans is understood in a biblical way, the serious problems with the Arminian scheme begin to emerge in our consciousness. Human responsibility is predicated on there being someone to whom you are responsible. The argument that I am not responsible unless some aspect of my being is completely outside the governance of God is false; that is the very basis of not having responsibility.

This was, in part, why Abram expressed himself as he did in Genesis 15 concerning Eliezer standing in line as his heir. But the reality of God choosing who is and is not in his covenant family is clearly seen and taught in Scripture. God worked supernaturally through a "natural" process that he had created and providentially superintended in order to produce Isaac. Abraham believed in God and this meant *believing what God would do* (Romans 4:13–25). Yes, this meant Abraham doing something. Yes, faith and obedience to God go hand in hand. Do not overlook what a "normal" or "natural" thing it was that constituted Abraham's grand obedience—having sex with Sarah.[15] Still, it was God who brought about a particular result.

As we move further in Scripture we get more details regarding the centrality of the family in God's plan for creation and redemption. The Israelites, whom God rescues from Egypt, are regarded as God's children. It is through them that God is fulfilling his covenant promise to Abraham, Isaac, and Jacob that began with Adam and was maintained miraculously through Noah (Exod 2:23; Gen 11:26; 5:32). Genesis details the family lines of God's people Israel. They are both biological and *supernatural*. While there is a distinction to be made between these categories, the Bible does not in an ultimate sense set these categories off against each other, but presents them as integrated with each other.[16] The God who created all is really and personally present in creation and con-

15. The Bible does not warrant that every Christian has to be engaged in some sort of "extreme" or "radical" activity in order to be used by God for the advancement of his kingdom. Much of the pandering after the "spectacular" or "extreme" or "radical" in certain strains of American Christianity is simply a reflection of how Platonic-like such people's thinking has become (they operate with a hierarchy of spirituality and do not recognize the eternal and spiritual significance of the normal routines of life). Again, they have fundamentally failed to discern an existing integration.

16. Protestant Liberal theology—going back to Rene Descartes and Baruch Spinoza, proliferated in modern biblical criticism in Europe during the eighteenth century, and popularized through Friedrich Schleiermacher and the German Liberal theologians of the nineteenth century—failed to understand and bow to this truth. In important ways, Arminian theology and Roman Catholicism fail to understand it as well, and operate along the same lines of thought as Protestant Liberalism. Where the proper distinction between God and creation are not maintained, one either considers God as *dissolved* into creation, which amounts to pantheistic mysticism, or regards God as *disconnected* from creation, which amounts to deistic rationalism. That there is a substantive connection between nineteenth-century Protestant Liberalism and much of contemporary American evangelicalism can be seen, among other ways, in the popularization within both of the sloganeering question "What would Jesus do?" See chapter 2 for a fuller treatment of these matters.

trols it to accomplish purposes that cannot be confined to, or regarded as merely the product of, humans exercising powers latent to the creation. When God commanded Israel to love him with all that they are, to have his words on their heart and to teach their children diligently all his words—to talk of them when they sit, walk, lie down and rise up, to bind them on their hands, to have them as frontlets between their eyes, and to write them on the doorposts of their houses—he revealed that such teaching concerned the totality of life (Deut 6:4–9). Thus, the biological and redemptive families were already integrated with God's truth. The entire book of Proverbs is testimony to the responsibility both parents have in life instruction that is integrated to God's saving purpose for his children.[17] Abraham's children were not only his biological offspring but also the many others who came to believe in the God of Abraham through the *instruction of his family in doing righteousness and justice.* The "children of Abraham" are all those who believe in the God of Abraham for salvation, and they are the church of the Lord Jesus Christ—both Jew and Gentile. This is precisely Paul's point in Galatians 3.[18] The centrality of the union between the biological family and the supernatural family of God, the Church, can also be seen in the New Testament.

Our purpose is not to give an exhaustive study, but it is important to see that the New Testament continues and, indeed, brings to fulfillment the emphasis of the family for Christian thinking and living. The New Testament is replete with this emphasis[19]—Ephesians 5:21—6:4, Colossians 3:18–21, 1 Thessalonians 2:1–12, 1 Timothy 3:1–7, and 1 Peter 5:1–5, in particular, help us see that the tender, nurturing, and patient diligence of parents—both fathers and mothers—is to be the means through which children are to be discipled/educated (do not think narrowly here). Of course, God, by providing all that we need for life, is both our empowering source and our example, and his people are to reflect his character in what they say and do.[20]

17. Ps 78 not only calls for this but also performs it.

18. Romans 4 and 11 and Ephesians 2 make the point as well. So, too, did Jesus in a different way in John 8. It is also made by the Apostle Peter in Acts 3 and 4.

19. For example, Matt 23:30, 32; Luke 1:17, 55, 72; 6:23, 26; 11:47–48; John 4:20; 6:31, 49, 58; numerous verses in the book of Acts; Rom 9:5; 11:28; 15:8; 1 Cor 4:15; 10:1; Eph 6:4; Col 4:21; and 1 John 2:13–14, among others.

20. For only a representative list: Matt 6:8–13; 7:7–11; 10:17–33; 11:25–30; 12:50; 18:1–35; Luke 12:22–34; 22:24–30; John 1:14–18; 5:17–47; 6:27–65; 8:18–56; 10:15–38; 14:6–17:25 (this section explicitly emphasizes the Trinitarian nature of redemption and

FAMILY AS THE TEMPLATE FOR ALL SOCIAL RELATIONS

If you know what Scripture says about the biological family, and how it reflects God, you know what it means for the church to operate as the church, because it is the biological family that is the miniature replica of the Church. As Jonathan Edwards said many years ago, echoing the truth that was understood quite well by many Christians of his era, "Every family is a little church." Satan's attempt at destroying the church is perhaps approached most effectively from his attempt to destroy the presence, or at least prominence, of the biological family. Just as it is true that every family is a little church, it is also true that every church is a family. In fact, Scripture teaches that every formally organized human social structure is to be regarded as a "family," with all involved recognizing that they fulfill the functions of father or mother or children—or, as it used to be understood, of "superiors" and "inferiors."[21] It is not surprising, at least to us, that at a time when there is a significant splintering of the biological family, there is also a corresponding stress felt in churches and Christian schools. To the degree that biological fathers, first and foremost, and secondarily biological mothers, fail to understand and fulfill their duties and privileges, the church and all Christian endeavors experience failure. Unless modified by the term *biological*, we will, through the remainder of this chapter, refer to those in authority as parent(s) and those whom they are to serve (and who are to submit to their authority) as child(ren). Age has nothing to do with these designations.

TO UNDERMINE GOD'S AUTHORITY STRUCTURE
IS TO UNDERMINE HIS PURPOSES

Sinners who are working at not retaining God in their thinking (Romans 1:18–32) will do all they can to suppress truth regarding the biological family and its central role in revealing God and advancing God's kingdom. One can perhaps understand, then, why many who climb the lad-

---

thus unites the Holy Spirit's work to God the Father); Acts 1:4; 1 Thess 2:11; 1 Tim 3:1–7; Heb 12:7–13; 13:7–8; Jas 1:17–27; 1 John 2:1—3:3; 2 John 1:9–11. (Note that the latter text not only emphasizes the relationship of the Father to the Son, but also both as only possessed by us when we remain in the *teachings* or *doctrine* regarding the Father and Son, and thereby the Holy Spirit.)

21. If one wants some serious material regarding how one should perhaps begin thinking along these lines, consider what the Westminster Larger Catechism, Questions and Answers 124–132, have to say about these matters.

der in educational institutions while amassing academic degrees in the formal discipline of education are some of the most confused and unhelpful theologians. Such institutions, some of which identify themselves as Christian, have adopted a view of education that is largely predicated on non-Christian and statist goals that deny the biblical teaching regarding God and the biological family and attempt to weaken, if not destroy, the bond between parent and child. The whole approach in American government-funded and government-operated schools disconnects children from their biological parents and can significantly undermine the biological parent's role in the child's life. Its effect is to give them new "parents" by teaching a dogma that orients the child to the mass public culture that helps make them a "good citizen."[22] This was *always* the intent, at least by some, who pushed for federally funded and state-run schools in the latter part of the nineteenth century.[23] While this may not be the stated or self-conscious intent of some, if not many, in such schools, nonetheless that was the intent of those who devised the operational structure. Our concern is the actual operational structure and its effect, not the sincere intentions of those involved in it.

Unfortunately, because even Christians retain sin in this life, Christians are not immune to avoiding the truth regarding the biological family. The confusion and competing interests that exist among Christians both in their educational and ecclesiastical pursuits, and that

22. The history of state and federally funded education reveals the statist goals of American public education. Richard A. Baer Jr., "American Public Education and the Myth of Value Neutrality," in *Democracy and the Renewal of Public Education*, 3, rightly affirmed the point made by John E. Coons almost thirty years ago that identifying schools in America as "public" and "private" is quite misleading. It has been and continues to be more accurate to identify them as "government" and "nongovernment" schools. What most people regard as "local" schools are, functionally speaking, run by state and government agencies.

23. The American initiative has paralleled and been inspired in important ways by educational developments in Germany but was generally fueled by the principles of the atheistic strains of the Enlightenment. For background on these matters, see Dawson, *The Crisis of Western Education*; Gay, *The Enlightenment: An Interpretation, The Rise of Modern Paganism*; Gay, *The Enlightenment: An Interpretation, The Science of Freedom*; Gay, *The Cultivation of Hatred*; Marsden, *The Soul of the American University*. The ubiquity of these issues is difficult to avoid in any reputable history of the United States and its relationship to the broader currents of Western intellectual thought. For a clear biblical jeremiad against the ascendancy of government-funded and government-run schools in the early portion of the twentieth century, see Machen, *Education, Christianity, and the State*.

mark much of the American evangelical landscape, are organically related to the ignorance that marks many of them regarding the character
and function of the biological family.[24]

SOME IMPLICATIONS OF THE FATHERS
AND MOTHERS PARADIGM

In *Family-Based Youth Ministry*, Mark DeVries articulated the fundamental problem with paying lip service to the importance of fathers and
mothers, and operating a biblical ministry to youth that pulled them
away from their parents and generally isolated them with their peers.[25]
In short, it may make such teens good youth group members, but it generally leaves them with little sense of their God-created relationship and
responsibility to both their parents and the Church. While God may
have blessed various ministries constructed on the model of segregat-
ing teenagers into their own niche group, that blessing by itself is no
indication that the model is mandated by Scripture. At various times
throughout his people's history, God has blessed *despite, not because of,*
his people's obvious departure from biblically mandated ways of operating.[26] The stress on the vital role that our biological parents have in our
discipleship to the Lord Jesus does not warrant a model that is simply
for the "crisis of the hour." The youth-group model of ministry that has
prevailed in most American churches from the 1950s to today has never
been the biblical ideal, nor will it ever be. In fact, it often mirrors what
has been done in government-run schools for decades. While we would
stop short of calling it inherently sinful, it is hardly the biblical ideal.

The chief responsibility that a husband and wife have in life is to
each other, and this flows into any children with which the Lord chooses

---

24. All the talk and literature about "doing" church, and the forays into different
"approaches," reveals an ignorance of the clear teaching of Scripture and the simplicity
of God's order. That is not to say that there will not be room for creativity in the sorts of
ministries that develop among various churches. Still, whatever forms those ministries
take, they will function under the authority of men who demonstrate that they understand what it means to be godly fathers, and the women involved will demonstrate
that they understand what it means to be godly mothers. Such men and women do
not necessarily need to be married to understand and fulfill these realities, because
their origin and example is seen in God in his relationship to his people, not first and
foremost in human experience.

25. DeVries, *Family-Based Youth Ministry.*

26. This is one of the themes of the book of Judges.

to bless them. This is how their relationship to God is primarily worked out. Among other things, this means the following. Biblically faithful fathers and mothers love their children by providing them with what they need in life, both physically and spiritually. This means nourishing and protecting them so that they grow to the point of being able to live as faithful servants in God's kingdom. We live by every word that proceeds from the mouth of God (Deut 8:3; Matt 4:4). Therefore, a text such as 2 Timothy 3:16–17, which tells us what the word of God does for God's children, is a wonderful guide in helping us understand how we should think about what a faithfully biblical father and mother do in providing the spiritual nourishment and protection that will cultivate life in their children.[27] Teachers, coaches, board members, and administrators must have this as their model, because they are the "fathers" and "mothers" of every school.

The four things affirmed by Paul regarding what God's word is profitable for in 2 Timothy 3:16–17 form a chiasm in which he asserts a positive function, then two negative ones, and then a positive one. By "negative" we ought not to think of something bad but of something that negates so that, in the end, the result is positive. Thus, it is perhaps better to understand the chiasm in gardening terms—planting and pruning. Whatever analogy we use, one thing is certain: if we are to be parents who become like Jesus, He must be formed in us. Thus, God's Word must form us so that we can help form others for God's glory. This means that there is a family construct that drives how we operate as individuals and as a community. First, we look at the dynamic of family as it pertains to individual conduct, and then we think about it in relation to the functioning of the community.

Teaching

The godly parent/teacher being formed by God's profitable word is profitable for teaching. This is authoritative instruction first and foremost regarding the Scriptures, but secondarily this relates to every subject discipline because Jesus is Lord of all. Thus, 2 Timothy 3:16–17 is primarily addressing the preaching of God's word in the church, but is secondarily and organically related to all that we do and say as Christians. Among other things, the text of Scripture is a historical literary document that

27. See the helpful analysis in Knight, *The Pastoral Epistles*, 449–50.

addresses our entire view of reality. Every subject discipline is enmeshed in our understanding of Scripture. Every parent (again, this is not necessarily a biological parent) must be able to address how his or her subject discipline is related to understanding Scripture (see Appendix 1). In this sense, every parent must be interdisciplinary in his or her approach and able to help children see the connections across disciplines. This will greatly assist a parent in answering the proverbial "Why?" question. In fact, we heartily endorse the notion that a parent engage in the regular study of other subject disciplines in order to understand their organic union. We also heartily endorse the idea that a parent be ready *at all times* to explain why a particular truth is vitally important for life.[28] If a parent cannot do this with a particular lesson, then he or she should suspend teaching it until such knowledge and the means of articulating it are firmly fixed in his or her mind.

This is one reason why collaboration with colleagues in other subject disciplines is vital to the ongoing growth of a faculty. This requires time and space, and that means money. Faithful parent/administrators will see to it that their faculty is not bogged down with paperwork and activities that amount to little more than a good advertising campaign, but instead have the time to discuss substantive topics in an open and honest way. This takes courage. Parents who are seeking to protect their turf or their agenda are *not* open to truth. Pursuing truth means being willing to change. It means being ready to receive, not just to give. It means being willing to courageously give truth. That is an unavoidable, and frankly rather obvious, implication of having the responsibility to give authoritative instruction. Still, such giving is organically united to a prior and ongoing receiving.

The greatest investment to make in producing WMIs, or Weapons of Mass Instruction (which is what every parent worth his or her salt wants to become), is to allocate money for books, conferences, and classes that a parent wants to read or attend. Although there may be some value in bringing someone in for an entire faculty to listen to, the indispensable approach is to encourage the family to be fertile soil for learning. Of course, that means there will always be growth in such families, which results in changes. Administrators (including pastors)

---

28. This is not to say that a parent is at the mercy of everyone who asks the "Why" question. A parent must exercise wisdom in knowing how and when to answer such questions.

who think they can control or manage such growth are fools. They only succeed in killing it.

Reproof

Christian communities—churches, schools and parachurch ministries—that show serious reluctance to change are an oxymoron, and they lose the ability to be profitable for teaching that is biblical in any sense of the term. If the word of God resides at the center of a family—school, church, or biological—then the family remains receptive to both teaching and learning that inevitably lead to reproof, and that reproof bears healthy fruit that keeps the relationships among the members central to its focus on God's word. Thus, the godly classroom teacher, administrator, or household parent is regularly evaluating the condition of the relationships within the family for signs of growth and learning. When members of the family change so as to align themselves with God's word, then that is a sure sign of the activity of God's Spirit, and this brings with it the certainty and conviction of the truthfulness of God's word (2 Tim 3:14). Thus, God prunes us (John 15), and the godly parent embodies reproof as the organic fruit of teaching.

The godly parent formed by God's profitable word is profitable for reproof. No one is above being corrected. Of course, that is easy to say. It is another thing to enter into that truth, especially with those we respect highly and who have a position of authority. Young children often find it literally incredible that their parents could be wrong. In part, this is why all parents, but especially biological ones, have an enormous responsibility in the discharge of their duties. They are naturally trusted by the children in their care, and they commit a heinous sin when they violate that trust. But this is also why the relationship between parent and child can become ripe for all sorts of profound evil. These relationships are based on a trust established through position and competence. Yet, all involved are sinners; we are profoundly wrong, damaged, and corrupt.

Although I may speak factually accurate statements (and I had better), this does not mean that I fully understand the implications and applications of such statements or that I faithfully put them into practice. In short, we are all in need of reproof, always. Simply because we have been placed in a position of authority does not mean that we are beyond reproof, like bosses capable only of criticism. Just as we had better be ready to give reproof when it is needed, and in the way that it should be delivered, we had better be ready to receive it, too. All this requires humility, wisdom, and courage. The possession of these qualities, and thus the understanding and practice of them, is the fruit of God's Spirit. This is all about recognizing that there is a reality, namely, God and his creation, which exists regardless of our perceptions of it. This runs completely contrary to the fact/value split addressed in chapter 2.

It becomes very easy, especially when we are preoccupied with our sincerity, as so many people are in the West (including, if not especially, many confessing Christians), for our light to become darkness (Matt 6:23). This is why we chose the Schlatter quote above. It is very easy for every kind of family to inoculate itself against God's word in the name of loyalty to God's word. When parents equate being a good Christian primarily with being a good, loyal member of the "family," then God's word is violated. Often this loyalty is defined as not disrupting family "unity" and frequently is expressed in terms of the so very vital work that the family absolutely must accomplish for God. Often, one hears concerns such as the following: "Souls are being lost to hell, why are we wrangling over these things?" and "Your questions and comments will disrupt the family unity." God's word is equated with a rather narrow and finite understanding of it, and those possessing this understanding remain unreceptive to hearing any challenge or correction to their most cherished applications of God's word. They equate their understanding of how God's word ought to be applied with the fundamental truth affirmation made by God's word. This is a heinous sin. Unfortunately, it does not remain even this simple, because such faulty notions are always enmeshed in a web of economic, political, and personal interests that can be woven by people so that they take the moral high ground. When this takes place, the prophet who calls them to repentance is the "disturber of Israel," the disturber of the peace. That prophet is often marginalized or removed altogether. When we remain resistant to reproof we embody the very antithesis of Jesus' disciples. The godly parent embraces and embodies reproof, which means he or she is regularly receiving it.

Correction

Those who embrace and embody reproof receive correction, and it forms them so that they behave righteously. When I receive reproof from others who speak the right interpretation of God's word to me, then I can be corrected and can bear fruit. The correction Paul has in mind is primarily a correction in behavior. Reproof and correction are all about receiving, listening, and observing. We can even receive reproof and correction without anyone directly speaking to us. By observing our children, we can and should see in them sins that we have cultivated. This is one of the chief ways that being a parent—biological or spiritual—is a blessing. I am able to see the fruit of my labor. That fruit is filled with my sin in some way.

Good coaches experience this when they see their athletes fail to execute particular actions that they should have learned from their coaches. The good coach is willing to admit how his or her coaching contributed to the problem. Show me a coach who yells a lot during a competition, and I will show you a coach who is not doing what he or she should do in practice. Show me a teacher who complains consistently about his or her students, and I will show you an incompetent teacher. The coach and teacher ought to recognize that when their athletes and students are evaluated through competitions, tests, quizzes, and essays, they too are evaluated. I (David) always take the perspective that if I am doing my job and my students are doing theirs, then I *ought to see* extremely high scores on tests, not because the test is too easy, but because the students are *prepared* for that for which they *ought to be* prepared. I would always look at the performance of my students or athletes as an evaluation of my teaching and coaching. Obviously, you have to distinguish between your responsibilities and the responsibilities of those you teach and coach, but a parent ought to have the perspective that if his or her child is not demonstrating a particular behavior, it is very likely because the parent has not taught him or her. The rather frightening truth is: Children are, *for the most part*, a reflection of their parents. This is why, if you want to see a correction in children, you address the need for correction among their parents.

Yes, sometimes people go their own way and are not receptive to learning. That is always possible. But even then, one needs to consider that perhaps the problem is that insufficient time has been spent cultivating the relationship with that person. Show me an administrator who is having difficulties with the faculty, or a school whose board members, administrators, and teachers are experiencing significant friction, and I will show you a school where the mission is not clear, where there is poor communication, where there is a lack of trust and a lack of concern for meeting people's needs. In short, there is a lack of leadership because there is a lack of love. We do not love by words alone, but in deeds. When a parent shows that he or she is willing to receive correction, it makes it a *whole lot* easier for a child to receive correction. In fact, what I have noticed in my marriage and with my own children is that when I am willing to admit that I have sinned or have simply made a mistake, and am willing to receive correction, then my wife and children are very responsive to any teaching that I presume to bring. God's word brings that correction, makes us willing and able to receive correction, and then equips us to know how to deliver it so that, both in us and in those we serve, God's righteousness is put on display.

Righteousness

God's word is not simply about telling us what *not* to do, but what *to do*. Organically related to this, though, is its equipping us how to think. The term for repentance in the New Testament is *metanoia*, which literally means "change of mind or thought." Perhaps many people are made nervous by this because (ironically) they *think* incorrectly about human thinking. Thus, they need to repent about their understanding of repentance. Human thinking is organically related to human actions. Changed thinking *is* changed behavior. Want to know what you really believe? Observe what you do.[29] Thus, God's Word directs our thinking and behavior simultaneously, or it directs neither. Of course, the symmetry is not exact or perfect in this life, because of sin. Still, there truly is an organic relation between the two. The parent feasting on God's word will affirm biblical doctrine and demonstrate, to some degree, biblical or righteous behavior.

Righteous parents love the whole family and sacrifice for it so that its members are nourished in God's righteous ways. So, righteous parents are about nourishing their relationships in the family so that each family member understands who he or she is in Jesus, and how Jesus is calling him or her to lifelong discipleship with him that results in righteous behavior. Righteous parents model what this looks like by teaching, reproving, and correcting. Righteous parents realize that history is moving and changing, so they do not resort to trite mantras spouted over and over again that communicate that they are not thinking substantively about how the changing realities of life ought to be responded

---

29. Jesus makes this clear in Matt 7:15–20.

to by God's righteous servant.[30] Righteous parents pray with and for their children and regularly speak of how God's word is to be applied, because God's word is applicable to life. Righteous parents also recognize that there is a power in what they do that far exceeds what they can merely say. This is why righteous parents are concerned not simply with their sincerity and good intentions, but with their actual obedience to God's word. Righteous parents are very concerned with how they treat people and how others respond to them. Righteous parents are very concerned about their attitudes and motives being out of accord with what they believe and what they do. Righteous parents grieve over their sin and its effect on others.

Righteous parents demonstrate what it means to spend time and money learning God's word, meeting the needs of God's people, first and foremost, and loving their neighbors. This is worship of God. Righteous parents live joyously because they know the One who is worth rejoicing over. Righteous parents make a joyful noise to the Lord. Righteous parents demonstrate what it means to utilize the gifts God has given them, and to live in a balanced way. Righteous parents bow to God's order of fulfilling biological family responsibilities first and seeing these in relation to the church. Righteous parents are not stretched too thin because they fully understand that God and his kingdom are not dependent on them. Righteous parents rest, and others rest in their presence. Righteous parents laugh because of the inherent humor in life and the glorious victory already accomplished by God. Righteous parents recognize that God's righteousness does not find a ready welcome in the world, and so are ready to be persecuted for righteousness' sake. Righteous parents receive persecution even among confessing Christians, because the enemies of righteousness often take their stand inside the community of God's people and must be resisted. Righteous parents are wise to all of this.

---

30. I think of a former colleague whose response to "How are you?" was virtually always the same cliché of an answer. It was very difficult for me to maintain a genuine concern for the brother because he was communicating a lack of transparency and a failure to think substantively about himself in relation to obviously new circumstances. It was also a rather insulting way to respond to intelligent and genuinely concerned brothers and sisters in Christ. Not surprisingly, I had numerous students come to me and complain about how infuriating his classes could be, because he would not listen to them. I understood.

Family Functioning

It is not enough to think about what we should be doing as individuals in terms of our moral conduct if we do not see how it is integral to functioning as a community. The truth that these features are *personal*, finding their fullest manifestation in a person, the Lord Jesus, means that one's personal moral conduct is organically woven into a community. There is a collaborative, communal aspect to biblical teaching and learning. Whereas in government-run schools this is all about shaping everyone so that they become good citizens—worshipers of the state and proponents of its dogma—Christian educational endeavors, whether in a school or home, ought to be for the purpose of shaping individuals to be mature adults who are like Jesus. Fundamentally, this means recognizing to whom you are responsible and fulfilling your duty to them. Jesus did not save individuals to live apart from others, as isolated as islands. God has always been about saving a family, a community, and that community has one faith, one hope, one baptism, and one Spirit, because it has one Father (Eph 4:4-6).

Central to this is the responsibility of biological parents to their children. Thus, a Christian community of learning forces parents to deal with their children and children with their parents. The school does not function as a substitute for the biological parents, as it does in government-run schools. Rather, the school is a place where the biological parents are present and directly governing what is taught, how it is taught, and what is done and not done across the entire spectrum of activities and procedures. Yet, this cannot be done unless everyone is confessing the same fundamental doctrinal truths, which presupposes clearly expressing those truths and giving anyone wanting to be involved in the educational community the opportunity to do the same. Interdenominational Christian schools functionally communicate relativism in important ways, because they have in principle affirmed that the truth about the most vital doctrines of the Christian faith cannot really be known. They often functionally teach that every Christian only has his or her perceptions of such truths. It ought to go without saying that mom and dad have to be teaching the same things or the children are going to be very conflicted. Current home-school endeavors or church-based schools that adhere to one common confession are preferable to interdenominational enterprises. Even still, if a home-school or church-based enterprise does not clearly communicate the expressed doctrinal positions of those who differ from them, they are guilty of bearing false witness. Thus, a school adhering to Reformed theology and the Westminster Confession of Faith that does not accurately explain the content of Arminianism is bearing false witness. The same is obviously true with the school adhering to Arminian beliefs in their teaching; they must accurately teach what is expressed by those who disagree with them. Otherwise, you do not have scholarship, but propaganda. But make no mistake about it, parents will take a stand on such matters; you cannot punt.

The fact that the biological parents are to be present and not to be substituted for does not mean that every parent must be directly involved in giving instruction on all subject matters. It does mean that a parent will know what is taught and be able to engage with his or her child regarding such content so that both will mature in their understanding of what that content has to do with them individually and with their place in God's kingdom. I do not have to be an expert mathematician to converse with others about math. Math is not my primary calling, but I do use it, and it is related to all that I do. Thus, my ability to speak with my children about math or anything else strengthens my bond with them and can assist them in seeing who I am as an individual and who they are in relation to the mission of the church. This is not a myopic approach to the biological family but one that recognizes the organic ties that the biological family has to the spiritual family. No biological family is an end in itself.

Naturally, all this calls into question the pursuit and use of finances. Because the current operation of most Christian schools mirrors that of government-run schools, there is often an enormous waste of financial resources, at least when set within and compared with the approach that we advocate. Again, if the current success of home-school scenarios does not teach traditional, government-run modeled advocates this lesson, then they have become Uncle Andrews, and are still pretending that the Emperor has new clothes. By reorganizing in a way that is in keeping with what we advocate, more can be taught in less time, by a greater array of experts in their fields, with less money. The goal of this reorganization is nurturing people for the kingdom of God, which will clearly contrast with what is taking place in government-run schools. Among other things, this will mean fewer administrators will be needed. The number of administrators in education increases the more one operates in accord with humanistic approaches. We advocate not the eradication of administration, but the streamlining of it.

CONCLUSION

At the heart of God's creation and his rescue of creation from sin is the biological family. We must understand this if we are to understand a faithfully biblical view of education. A biblical focus on the family has both individual and corporate implications for Christian educational endeavors. Unfortunately, because most Christian schools functionally operate like government-run schools, they are actually communicating some of the same unbiblical beliefs of those government-run schools, and functionally denying the basic doctrine they claim is true. When the biblical doctrine of the family is understood and faithfully responded to it will lead to a revolution regarding how Christian educational practices take place. This does not necessarily mean the eradication of the Christian school, but it will mean significant overhauling of it. That overhauling can and should take place, because God the Father is at work redeeming his people from sin through his Son by his Spirit. Thus, the sins of God's people need to be confessed—turned from—and a new way adopted for its learning endeavors. This is so the distinct character of Jesus is seen, not only in the doctrine we confess and the conduct of our individual lives but also in how we function as a community. Thus, the world will see that the body of Christ functions as a family that derives its definition, purpose, and wholeness from God the Father, Son, and Holy Spirit.

Unscientific Postscript

WE HOPE AND PRAY that this book was challenging and edifying to you and that it will be used by God to stimulate Christian growth, both at an individual and an institutional level. Again, we would like to reiterate that we are not denouncing all Christian schools or the administration, faculty, and staff that work in them. Indeed, one of the reasons for this book is the unnecessary burden that we perceive many very gifted, highly intelligent, and self-sacrificing people in Christian education operate under. We are certainly not making judgments about the eternal state of those with whom we disagree or criticize. Rather, it is our goal to point out some of the inconsistencies and incoherencies that have plagued, hindered, and hurt Christian education in the West over the past half-century. We are not perfect, and we do not claim to have figured out everything pertaining to learning and teaching. We, too, continue to struggle with many of the ideas and practices that we criticized. We know that we were, at times, stern in our criticism of certain ideas and practices. If you were in any way offended by what we wrote, we encourage you to consider why you were offended. It could be that your sin was called onto the table, and that offended you. If that is the case, we make no apologies. Frankly, we called *our sin* onto the table. When writing about many of the attitudes or actions that we criticized, all we had to do was think about ourselves and recall what we have found ourselves doing all too easily. As brothers and sisters in Christ, it is our responsibility to hold each other accountable for sin. We are not attempting to take the moral high ground here. We are very much open to dialoguing with others on these matters. If we have needlessly offended, please forgive us. Our desire is not only to help others in the kingdom become better teachers but also to become better teachers ourselves.

Although it has already been stated, it bears repeating that there is no single right way of organizing and operating a Christian school. There are many different contexts and circumstances, owing to many variables, that will impact how a Christian school can and should function. Still, there are guiding biblical principles that must be applied to the various milieus in which Christian schools exist. The final three chapters of this book sought to provide some of the most basic of these guiding biblical principles; applying them to your particular situation is the responsibility of your school community at large. Administration, faculty, and staff must meet and converse to discern *how* these biblical principles apply to your school. Decisions must be made prayerfully and with careful deliberation and biblical discernment. Becoming and/or remaining faithful to the scriptural witness concerning the nature and purpose of human learning will not be easy, and, in many cases, it will necessitate systemic change. It may require some schools to shut down or merge with others. It may require the elimination of certain positions and/or the addition of others. It may be necessary to shift personnel to new departments and new responsibilities. It may mean that some teachers and/or school families leave over fundamental differences in philosophy. Indeed, this sort of systemic change is downright frightening. But the only fear that ought to influence what we do is the fear of the Lord. If we are going to have definitively Christian schools or learning communities, we must be honest with ourselves as individuals and institutions. We must have the courage to admit when, where, and how we are wrong, so that individually and institutionally we may repent and live obediently to the Lord.

Applying the biblical guiding principles presented in this book requires you to discern your current situation. Where is your school right and where is it wrong? Where is it strong? Where is it in need of work? You must recognize that the application of biblical truth cannot occur without the help and power of the Holy Spirit, and so you and your school must pray earnestly for the Holy Spirit's sanctifying work in every area of your school and in the churches that feed it. Moreover, applying these principles necessitates a right understanding of Scripture. You must prayerfully wrestle with the text and consult pastors and theologians if and when you get "stuck." Ultimately, you and your school must have an unswerving commitment to being obedient to the word of God.

We are happy to help you and your school in this endeavor in any way that we can. We hope to post articles and brief comments regularly on our website. Additionally, we are available for consultation and speaking engagements; please visit our website (www.oldschoolnewclothes. com) for more information.

Truly, there is much more that can and should be said. This book is simply an introduction. All of its chapters are merely touching upon the topics addressed. Our hope and prayer is that by having done so we have touched the Christian community in a place and to a degree that it might respond with growth, so that we all might grow together in the grace and knowledge of our Lord and serve him more faithfully.

Appendix

Part of the Christian Theological and Philosophical Root System for the Humanities

1. Every educational pursuit is governed by and rooted in a particular definition of knowledge and an ultimate goal for the use of that knowledge.

2. Definitions of knowledge must include beliefs about the nature of the human knower and the objects or subjects known by the knower.

3. How we think we acquire knowledge, what we consider worthy of knowing, and the purpose for which we acquire knowledge are integral to every educational pursuit.

4. All educational pursuits reveal either that humans are to be considered as their own end, or that humans are subservient to someone or something greater than themselves. As a result, all educational pursuits are religious or theological in nature. We either make ourselves the god we worship or serve, or we worship the Triune God of Scripture.

5. Since the Bible is a written document that took approximately fifteen hundred years to write and compile, the study of human language, history, and the nature of historical knowledge are integral to a well-informed understanding of the Bible.

6. The Bible is the ultimate authority for all knowledge claims, and thus there is, in a biblically Christian conception of human knowledge, a circularity that the Bible endorses, and regarding which it serves as the ultimate authority. This is so because God is ultimately the object of all human knowledge and ultimately the means by which humans know.

7. God created Man, male and female, in his own image, with the capacity to receive revelation from him through their five senses and their capacity to reason. Creation is revelation from God, as is his written word, the Bible, which is comprised of the Old and the New Testament. The consummate revelation of God is his Son, the Lord Jesus Christ, the Second Person of the Trinity. All this revelation is necessary for humans to know and fulfill the purpose God has for them, which is to be fruitful, multiply, fill the earth, and subdue it on God's behalf.

8. Humans were created with ability to acquire reliable knowledge from the created order through the use of their five senses and ability to reason. Though these capacities are corrupted and distorted by sin, humans can still acquire enough reliable knowledge to hold them accountable for their sin, and to allow them to live within the creation. All human reasoning is an exercise in interpretation, and this has never been done without faith commitments. Therefore, it is not biblical to think that reason takes us to a certain epistemological point *and then* faith kicks in, so to speak. Rather, all human reasoning is filled with faith commitments.

9. The following definition of human knowledge is consistent with Scripture: Human knowledge is the acquisition of an understanding of a person, object, or concept that corresponds to what God made that person or object to be and do—or what that concept means within God's revelation—and leads, in some degree, to the person obeying God.

10. The time and space realm in which humans live is not eternal. Rather, it has its beginning in the creative act of the Triune God speaking, and reaches its God-ordained purpose as God's revelation continues to go forth in and through it.

11. Time and space, as humans experience them, are sustained, governed, interpreted, or judged by God. Under the Triune God's providence, they are moving toward his ordained goal for them. From a biblically Christian perspective, any knowledge claim that is truly historical acknowledges rather than tries to hide or obscure God's sovereignty in and over creation and his supervision of history.

12. A biblically Christian view of language and history operates with the belief that God has revealed himself in the space-time realm that he created, as the Word that became flesh (John 1:1–14).

13. Both Christian and non-Christian epistemologies acknowledge the importance of language, and therefore human culture, in the knowing process and for knowledge claims.

14. In a biblically Christian epistemology, human culture and language have a role of *influence*, while in all non-Christian epistemologies, human culture and language have a *determinative* role. As a result, in all non-Christian epistemologies, human knowledge can be thought of as nothing more than the perceptions of the knower and the words the knower chooses to use to express such perceptions.

15. All non-Christian epistemologies lack the means to evaluate and judge competing knowledge claims. As a result, there is no epistemological basis for educational pursuits in non-Christian systems of knowing, and all non-Christian educational pursuits degenerate into some form of socialistic pragmatism or privatized self-interest.

16. The study of and acquisition of knowledge in any language and in any aspect of history highlights our use of language and the entire spectrum of human activity. Educational pursuits in language and history that deny or ignore the theological nature of any subject obscure the most fundamental character of the subject, and therefore offer little hope of rightly understanding the subject.

17. It is not always or obviously clear even to the most faithful Christian historians how God's ordained goals are being accomplished in and through human life and history. Still, God clearly reveals his commands for human life. These commands are the basis for all good human behavior and pursuits. The blessing that comes from God alone is the energizing source of any person or community's ability to practice such commands. These commands should become the starting point by which historians, who are faithful to the Bible, can discern God's good providences. Some of these good providences may not be discerned by God's people until many years after they have occurred. Some bad consequences of human activities may

not be identified, or their effects may not be measured, until many years after they have occurred.

18. Since the Bible reveals that there is a powerful evil being who seeks to corrupt, distort, and destroy God's work by disguising himself as an angel of light, the faithfully Christian historian will take great pains not to fall prey to simplistic or quick analyses of history.

19. God has ordained that he would be accessed primarily through a written text that can be read silently, or out loud, and verbally proclaimed. Therefore, reading and listening are emphasized by God as vitally important activities in our fulfillment as humans, or our redemption from sin. Moreover, learning how to express oneself verbally and in written form for the purposes of explanation and persuasion is not simply an activity for elite educational settings, but is integral to the development of every person who has the capacity for these activities. Still, each individual's capabilities will establish the boundaries for what he or she is able to accomplish in theses disciplines.

20. Humans are historical and social creatures who must understand themselves to be part of a historical process and particular communities in order to understand who they are and what they are obligated to do. Therefore, learning about the individuals and ideas of the past who have affected the development of various communities, including our own, and wrestling with our understanding of these individual and ideas within educational communities through writing and speaking is vital to knowing who we are and fulfilling our God-ordained duties.

Bibliography

Anselm. *Proslogion with the replies of Gaunilo and Anselm*. Indianapolis: Hackett, 1995.

Appleby, Joyce, Lynn Hunt, and Margaret Jacob. *Telling the Truth about History*. New York: Norton, 1994.

Baer, Richard A., Jr. "American Public Education and the Myth of Value Neutrality." In *Democracy and the Renewal of Public Education: Essays*, edited by Richard John Neuhaus, 1–24. Grand Rapids: Eerdmans, 1987.

Bassett, W. Philip, and Eddie K. Baumann. "Teaching Methodologies." In *Foundations of Christian School Education*, edited by James Braley, Jack Layman, and Ray White. Colorado Springs: Purposeful Design, 2003.

Baumann, Eddie K. "The Essentials of Integration: Developing the Image of God." *Christian School Education* 13 (2009/2010) 32–34.

Bavinck, Herman. *The Doctrine of God*. Translated by William Hendriksen. Carlisle, PA: Banner of Truth, 1977.

————. *In the Beginning: Foundations of Creation Theology*. Edited by John Bolt. Translated by John Vriend. Grand Rapids: Baker, 1999.

Beckwith, Francis, and J. P. Moreland. "Series Preface: A Call to Integration and the Christian Worldview Integration Series." In Paul D. Spears and Steven R. Loomis, *Education for Human Flourishing: A Christian Perspective*. Downers Grove, IL: InterVarsity, 2009.

Berkhof, Louis. *Systematic Theology*. Grand Rapids: Eerdmans, 1996.

Brown, Colin. *Jesus in European Protestant Thought, 1778–1860*. Studies in Historical Theology 1. Durham, NC: Labyrinth, 1985.

Brown, Jerry Wayne. *The Rise of Biblical Criticism in America, 1800–1870: The New England Scholars*. Middletown, CT: Wesleyan University Press, 1969.

Calvin, John. *Institutes of the Christian Religion*. Edited by John T. McNeill. Translated by Ford Lewis Battles. 2 vols. The Library of Christian Classics, vols. 20 and 21. Philadelphia: Westminster, 1960.

Carson, D. A. *Becoming Conversant With the Emerging Church: Understanding a Movement and Its Implications*. Grand Rapids: Zondervan, 2005.

————. *Christ and Culture Revisited*. Grand Rapids: Eerdmans, 2008.

————. "The Dangers and Delights of Postmodernism." *Modern Reformation* 12 (2003) 11–17.

————, editor. *From Sabbath to Lord's Day: A Biblical, Historical, and Theological Investigation*. 1982. Reprinted, Eugene, OR: Wipf & Stock, 2000.

Chamblin, J. Knox. *Paul and the Self: Apostolic Teaching for Personal Wholeness*. 1993. Reprinted, Eugene, OR: Wipf & Stock, 2002.

Claiborne, Shaine. *The Irresistible Revolution: Living as an Ordinary Radical*. Grand Rapids: Zondervan, 2006.

Collins, Jack C. *Genesis 1–4: A Linguistic, Literary, and Theological Commentary.* Phillipsburg, NJ: Presbyterian & Reformed, 2006.

Copleston, Frederick, SJ. *A History of Philosophy.* Vol. 6., *Wolff to Kant.* New York: Doubleday, 1985.

Dabney, Robert Lewis. *Lectures in Systematic Theology.* 1878. Reprinted, Carlisle, PA: Banner of Truth, 1996.

Dawson, Christopher, *The Crisis of Western Education.* Steubenville, OH: Franciscan University Press, 1989.

Dennison, William D. *A Christian Approach to Interdisciplinary Studies: In Search of a Method and Starting Point.* Eugene, OR: Wipf & Stock, 2007.

DeVries, Mark. *Family-Based Youth Ministry: Reaching the Been-There, Done-That Generation.* Downers Grove, IL: InterVarsity, 1994.

Dorrien, Gary. *The Making of American Liberal Theology: Idealism, Realism, & Modernity, 1900–1950.* Louisville: Westminster, 2003.

———. *The Making of American Liberal Theology: Imagining Progressive Religion, 1805–1900.* Louisville: Westminster, 2001.

Evans, Richard J. *In Defense of History.* New York: Norton, 1999.

Frame, John M. *The Doctrine of God.* Phillipsburg, NJ: Presbyterian & Reformed, 2002.

———. *The Doctrine of the Christian Life.* Phillipsburg, NJ: Presbyterian & Reformed, 2008.

———. *The Doctrine of the Knowledge of God.* Phillipsburg, NJ: Presbyterian & Reformed, 1987.

———. *The Doctrine of the Word of God.* Phillipsburg, NJ: Presbyterian & Reformed, 2010.

Frei, Hans W. *The Eclipse of the Biblical Narrative: A Study in Eighteenth and Nineteenth Century Hermeneutics.* New Haven: Yale University Press, 1974.

Gay, Peter. *The Cultivation of Hatred.* The Bourgeois Experience, Victoria to Freud 3. New York: Norton, 1993.

———. *The Enlightenment: An Interpretation.* 2 vols. New York: Knopf, 1966–69.

Gerrish, B. A. "Natural and Revealed Religion." In *The Cambridge History of Eighteenth-Century Philosophy,* edited by Knud Haakonssen, vol. 2, 641–65. Cambridge: Cambridge University Press, 2006.

Gundlach, Bradley J. "The Evolution Question at Princeton, 1845–1929." PhD diss., University of Rochester, 1995.

Gunton, Colin E. *The One, the Three and the Many: God, Creation, and the Culture of Modernity.* New York: Cambridge University Press, 1993.

Habermas, Ronald T. *Introduction to Christian Education and Formation: A Lifelong Plan for Christ-Centered Restoration.* Grand Rapids: Zondervan, 2008.

Harrisville, Roy A., and Walter Sundberg. *The Bible in Modern Culture: Theology and Historical-Critical Method from Spinoza to Kasemann.* Grand Rapids: Eerdmans, 1995.

Helseth, Paul Kjoss. *"Right Reason" and the Princeton Mind: An Unorthodox Proposal.* Phillipsburg, NJ: Presbyterian & Reformed, 2010.

Hess, Frederick M. *Education Unbound: The Promise and Practice of Greenfield Schooling.* Alexandria, VA: ASCD, 2010.

Hoffecker, W. Andrew. "Enlightenments and Awakenings: The Beginning of Modern Culture Wars." In *Revolutions in Worldview: Understanding the Flow of Western*

Thought, edited by W. Andrew Hoffecker. Phillipsburg, NJ: Presbyterian & Reformed, 2007.

Horton, Michael. "Are Churches Secularizing America?" *Modern Reformation* 17 (2008) 42–47.

Jacobs, Heidi Hayes. *Curriculum 21: Essential Education for a Changing World*. Edited by Heidi Hayes Jacobs. Alexandria, VA: ASCD, 2010.

Kelly, Douglas F. *Creation and Change: Genesis 1.1—2.4 In the Light of Changing Scientific Paradigms*. Fearn: Mentor, 1997.

———. *Systematic Theology: Grounded in Holy Scripture and Understood in the Light of the Church*. Fearn: Mentor, 2008.

Kelly, J. N. D. *Early Christian Doctrines* Rev. ed. New York: HarperCollins, 1978.

Kline, Meredith, G. *Kingdom Prologue: Genesis Foundations for a Covenantal Worldview*. Overland Park, KS: Two Age, 2000.

Knight, George W. *The Pastoral Epistles: A Commentary on the Greek Text*. Grand Rapids: Eerdmans, 1992.

Kuklick, Bruce. "On Critical History." In *Religious Advocacy and American History*, edited by D. G. Hart and Bruce Kuklick. Grand Rapids: Eerdmans, 1998.

Leff, Gordon. *Medieval Thought: St. Augustine to Ockham*. Baltimore: Penguin, 1962.

Leithart, Peter J. "Medieval Theology and the Roots of Modernity." In *Revolutions in Worldview: Understanding the Flow of Western Thought*, edited by W. Andrew Hoffecker. Phillipsburg, NJ: Presbyterian & Reformed, 2007.

Lemov, Doug. *Teach Like a Champion: 49 Techniques that Put Students on the Path to College*. San Francisco: Jossey-Bass, 2010.

Lewis, C. S. *The Abolition of Man*. New York: Macmillan, 1947.

———. *The Magician's Nephew, The Chronicles of Narnia, Book 1*. New York: HarperCollins, 1983.

"The Link: Christian History Today." *Christian History* 72 (2001) 51–54.

Linnemann, Eta. *Historical Criticism of the Bible: Methodology or Ideology?* Translated by Robert W. Yarbrough. Grand Rapids: Baker, 1990.

———. *Is There a Synoptic Problem?: Rethinking the Literary Dependence of the First Three Gospels*. Translated by Robert W. Yarbrough. Grand Rapids: Baker, 1992.

Luther, Martin. *Luther's Works*. Vol. 1, *Lectures on Genesis: Chapters 1-5*. St. Louis: Concordia, 1999.

McCosh, James. "Recent Works on Kant." *The Presbyterian and Reformed Review* 1:3 (1890) 425–40.

MacCullough, Martha E. "How to Develop a Teaching Model for World View Integration." Langhorne, PA: Philadelphia Biblical University School of Business and Leadership, 1999.

Machen, J. Gresham. "Christianity and Culture." *Princeton Theological Review* 11:1 (1913) 1–15.

———. *Christianity and Liberalism*. New York: MacMillan, 1923.

———. *Education, Christianity, and the State*. Edited by John W. Robbins. Unicoi, TN: The Trinity Foundation, 2004.

———. "The Necessity of the Christian School." In *J. Gresham Machen: Selected Shorter Writings*. Edited by D. G. Hart. Phillipsburg, NJ: Presbyterian & Reformed, 2004.

Maier, Gerhard. *Biblical Hermeneutics*. Translated by Robert W. Yarbrough. Wheaton, IL: Crossway, 1994.

Marsden, George. *The Outrageous Idea of Christian Scholarship.* New York: Oxford University Press, 1997.

———. *The Soul of the American University: From Protestant Establishment to Established Nonbelief.* New York: Oxford University Press, 1994.

Miller, Donald. *Blue Like Jazz: Nonreligious Thoughts on Christian Spirituality.* Nashville: Nelson, 2003.

Mountjoy, Stephen. "Heart and Mind: The Dance of Faith-Learning Integration: Confluence and Contradiction." *Christian School Education* 13 (2009/2010) 27.

Muller, Richard A. *Post-Reformation Reformed Dogmatics: The Rise and Development of Reformed Orthodoxy, ca. 1520 to ca. 1725.* 4 vols. 2nd ed. Grand Rapids: Baker Academic, 2003.

Nash, Ronald H. *Faith and Reason: Searching for a Rational Faith.* Grand Rapids: Zondervan, 1988.

Naugle, David K. *Worldview: The History of a Concept.* Grand Rapids: Eerdmans, 2002.

Neuhaus, Richard John, editor. *Democracy and the Renewal of Public Education.* Grand Rapids: Eerdmans, 1987.

Pearcey, Nancy. *Total Truth: Liberating Christianity from Its Cultural Captivity.* Wheaton, IL: Crossway, 2004.

Pelikan, Jaroslav. *The Christian Tradition: A History of the Development of Doctrine.* Vol. 1, *The Emergence of the Catholic Tradition (100–600).* Chicago: The University of Chicago Press, 1971.

———. *The Christian Tradition: A History of the Development of Doctrine.* Vol. 3, *The Growth of Medieval Theology (600-1300).* Chicago: University of Chicago Press, 1980.

Piper, John. *The Future of Justification: A Response to N. T. Wright.* Wheaton, IL: Crossway, 2007.

Postman, Neil. *Amusing Ourselves to Death: Public Discourse in the Age of Show Business.* New York: Penguin, 1983.

Rauhut, Nils Ch. *Ultimate Questions: Thinking About Philosophy.* New York: Penguin, 2004.

Sabatier, August. *Outlines of a Philosophy of Religion: Based on Psychology and History.* New York: Doran, 1923.

Schindler, Debbie. "The Ethos of a School Committed to Professional Development." *Christian School Education* 13 (2009/2010) 22–24.

Schlatter, Adolf. *Do We Know Jesus?: Daily Insights for the Mind and Soul.* Grand Rapids: Kregel, 2005.

Schlossberg, Herbert. *Idols for Destruction: The Conflict of Christian Faith and American Culture.* Wheaton, IL: Crossway, 1990.

Seeman, Bradley N. "Evangelical Historiography Beyond the 'Outward Clash': A Case Study on the Alternation Approach." *Christian Scholar's Review* 33 (2003) 95–124.

Sire, James. *The Universe Next Door: A Basic Worldview Catalog.* Downers Grove, IL: InterVarsity, 1997.

Sloan, Douglas. *Faith and Knowledge: Mainline Protestantism and American Higher Education.* Louisville: Westminster, 1994.

Smith, David P. *B. B. Warfield's Scientifically Constructive Theological Scholarship.* Evangelical Theological Society Monograph Series. Eugene, OR: Wipf & Stock, 2011.

―――. "B. B. Warfield, Systematic Theology and the Preacher's Task." *Presbyterion* 35:2 (2009) 95–115.

Spears, Paul, and Steven Loomis. *Education for Human Flourishing: A Christian Perspective.* Downers Grove, IL: InterVarsity, 2009.

Spinoza, Baruch. *A Theologico-Political Treatise and A Political Treatise.* Translated by R. H. M. Elwes. New York: Dover, 1951.

Stover, Del. "Reform School." *American School Board Journal* 195 (2008) 15–18.

Stumpf, Samuel Enoch. *Socrates to Sartre: A History of Philosophy.* 5th ed. New York: McGraw Hill, 1993.

Talero, Kathleen Park, and Arthur Talero. *Foundations in Microbiology: Fourth Edition.* New York: McGraw Hill, 2002.

Tatar, Maria, editor. *The Annotated Classic Fairy Tales.* New York: Norton, 2002.

Tillich, Paul. *A History of Christian Thought: From Its Judaic and Hellenistic Origins to Existentialism.* Edited by Carl E. Braaten. New York: Simon & Schuster, 1968.

Van Groningen, Gerard. *From Creation to Consummation.* Sioux Center, IA: Dordt College Press, 1996.

―――. *Messianic Revelation in the Old Testament.* Grand Rapids: Baker, 1990.

Warfield, B. B. "Apologetics." In *The Works of Benjamin Breckinridge Warfield.* Vol. 9, *Studies in Theology*, 3–21. New York: Oxford University Press, 1932.

―――. "Authority, Intellect, Heart." In *Selected Shorter Writings*, edited by John E. Meeter, vol. 2, 668–71. Phillipsburg, NJ: Presbyterian & Reformed, 1973.

―――. "The Biblical Idea of Revelation." In *The Works of Benjamin Breckinridge Warfield.* Vol. 1, *Revelation and Inspiration*, 3–34. 1927. Reprint Baker, 1991.

―――. "Calvin's Doctrine of God." In *The Works of Benjamin Breckinridge Warfield.* Vol. 5, *Calvin and Calvinism*, 151. New York: Oxford University Press, 1931.

―――. "Christianity and Our Times." In *Selected Shorter Writings*, edited by John E. Meeter, vol. 1, 46–50. Phillipsburg, NJ: Presbyterian & Reformed, 1970.

―――. "The Divine and Human in the Bible." In *Selected Shorter Writings*, edited by John E. Meeter, vol. 2, 542–48. Phillipsburg, NJ: Presbyterian & Reformed, 1973.

―――. "God's Providence Over All." In *Selected Shorter Writings*, edited by John E. Meeter, vol. 1, 110–15. Phillipsburg, NJ: Presbyterian & Reformed, 1970.

―――. "The Idea of Revelation and Theories of Revelation." In *The Works of Benjamin Breckinridge Warfield.* Vol. 1, *Revelation and Inspiration*, 37–48. 1927. Reprint Baker, 1991.

―――. "The Idea of Systematic Theology." In *The Works of Benjamin Breckinridge Warfield.* Vol. 9. *Studies in Theology*, 49–87. New York: Oxford University Press, 1932.

―――. "The Indispensableness of Systematic Theology to the Preacher." In *Selected Shorter Writings*, edited by John E. Meeter, vol. 2, 280–88. Phillipsburg, NJ: Presbyterian & Reformed, 1973.

―――. "Introduction to *Beattie's Apologetics*." In *Selected Shorter Writings*, edited by John E. Meeter, vol. 2, 668–71. Phillipsburg, NJ: Presbyterian & Reformed, 1973.

―――. "The Religious Element in the Preparation for the Ministry." *The Presbyterian Observer* (October 15, 1885). PTS Archives, Box 53.

―――. "A Review of *De Zekerheid Des Geloofs*." In *Selected Shorter Writings*, edited by John E. Meeter, vol. 2, 106–23. Phillipsburg, NJ: Presbyterian & Reformed, 1973.

―――. "The Right of Systematic Theology." In *Selected Shorter Writings*, edited by John E. Meeter, vol. 2, 219–79. Phillipsburg, NJ: Presbyterian & Reformed, 1973.

————. *Selected Shorter Writings.* Edited by John E. Meeter. 2 vols. Phillipsburg, NJ: Presbyterian & Reformed, 1973.

————. "The Task and Method of Systematic Theology." In *The Works of Benjamin Breckinridge Warfield.* Vol. 9. *Studies in Theology,* 91–105. New York: Oxford University Press, 1932.

————. "Theology A Science." In *Selected Shorter Writings,* edited by John E. Meeter, vol. 2, 207–12. Phillipsburg, NJ: Presbyterian & Reformed, 1973.

————. *The Works of Benjamin Breckinridge Warfield.* Vol. 4, *Studies in Tertullian and Augustine.* 1930. Reprint Baker, 1991.

Wells, David F. *Above All Earthly Pow'rs: Christ in a Postmodern World.* Grand Rapids: Eerdmans, 2005.

————.. *The Courage to Be Protestant.* Grand Rapids: Eerdmans, 2008.

————. *God in the Wasteland: The Reality of Truth in a World of Fading Dreams.* Grand Rapids: Eerdmans, 1994.

————. *Losing Our Virtue: Why the Church Must Recover Its Moral Vision.* Grand Rapids: Eerdmans, 1998.

————. *No Place for Truth: Or, Whatever Happened To Evangelical Theology?.* Grand Rapids: Eerdmans, 1993.

Wenham, Gordon J. *Genesis 1–15.* Word Biblical Commentary 1. Waco, TX: Word, 1987.

Wilkens, Steve, and Alan G. Padgett. *Christianity and Western Thought: A History of Philosophers, Ideas and Movements.* Vol. 2, *Faith and Reason in the Nineteenth Century.* Downers Grove, IL: InterVarsity, 2000.

Wilson, Douglas. *Recovering the Lost Tools of Learning: An Approach to Distinctively Christian Education.* Wheaton, IL: Crossway, 1991.

Wilson, Marvin R. *Our Father Abraham: Jewish Roots of the Christian Faith.* Grand Rapids: Eerdmans, 1989.

Wittmer, Michael E. *Heaven Is a Place on Earth: Why Everything You Do Matters to God.* Grand Rapids: Zondervan, 2004.

Yarbrough, Robert W. *The Salvation-Historical Fallacy?: Reassessing the History of New Testament Theology.* Leiden: Deo, 2004.

Young, Edward J. *Studies in Genesis One.* Philadelphia: Presbyterian & Reformed, 1964.

Zaspel, Fred G. *The Theology of B. B. Warfield: A Systematic Summary.* Wheaton, IL: Crossway, 2010.

Printed in the USA
CPSIA information can be obtained
at www.ICGtesting.com
LVHW020142251023
762044LV00004B/16